"*JEWels* is an invaluable contribution to
public, academic, Jewish, and non-Jewish
communities as both timeless archive and
profound cultural expression. Innumerable
moving narratives, provocative anecdotes,
age-old jokes, and sweet recollections reveal
the great range of meaning held in the daily
and deep verbal arts of Jewish tradition.
Above all, the raw poems, annotated with
commentary and questions for discussion,
compel readers to enter into illuminating
conversation with the individuals in this book
and one another."

—GABRIELLE A. BERLINGER, assistant professor of
American studies and folklore and Tanenbaum Fellow
in Jewish History and Culture at University of North
Carolina–Chapel Hill

JEWELS

UNIVERSITY OF NEBRASKA PRESS

LINCOLN

JEWels

Teasing Out the Poetry in Jewish Humor and Storytelling

EDITED BY *Steve Zeitlin*

LEAD COMMENTARY BY *Peninnah Schram*

WITH COMMENTARIES *by Robert J. Bernstein, Esther Cohen, Lisa Lipkin, Bob Mankoff, Flash Rosenberg, Jack Santino, Rabbi Edward Schecter, and Zev Shanken*

WITH CONTRIBUTIONS *by Dennis J. Bernstein, Robert J. Bernstein, Roslyn Bresnick-Perry, Esther Cohen, Sylvia Cole, Rachel Ray Faust, Robert Hershon, Bob Holman, Rabbi David Holtz, David Ignatow, Marc Kaminsky, Mayer Kirshenblatt, Barbara Kirshenblatt-Gimblett, Carol Klenfner, Jack Kugelmass, Annie Lanzillotto, Warren Lehrer, Philip Levine, Lisa Lipkin, Bob Mankoff, Linda Pastan, Flash Rosenberg, Jack Santino, Rabbi Edward Schecter, Peninnah Schram, Cherie Karo Schwartz, Renée Fodor Schwarz, Hal Sirowitz, Zev Shanken, Mark Solomon, Sparrow, Arthur Strimling, Marc Wallace, Rabbi Sheila Peltz Weinberg, Francine Witte, Lila Zeiger, Aaron Zeitlin, and Others*

THE JEWISH PUBLICATION SOCIETY

PHILADELPHIA

Acknowledgments for the use of copyrighted
material appear on page 263, which constitutes
an extension of the copyright page.

Library of Congress Cataloging-in-Publication Data
Names: Zeitlin, Steve J., editor. |
Schram, Peninnah, contributor.
Title: JEWels : teasing out the poetry in Jewish
humor and storytelling / edited by Steve Zeitlin;
lead commentary by Peninnah Schram.
Description: Lincoln : University of Nebraska Press,
[2023] | Includes bibliographical references and index.
Identifiers: LCCN 2022019670
ISBN 9780827615526 (paperback)
ISBN 9780827619005 (epub)
ISBN 9780827619012 (pdf)
Subjects: LCSH: Jewish poetry. | Jewish wit and humor. |
Jews—Anecdotes. | BISAC: POETRY / Anthologies (multiple
authors) | RELIGION / Inspirational | LCGFT: Poetry. | Humor.
Classification: LCC PN6109.5 .J49 2023 |
DDC 808.87/98924—dc23/eng/20220725
LC record available at https://lccn.loc.gov/2022019670

Set and designed in Adobe Text and Scala by N. Putens.

CONTENTS

ACKNOWLEDGMENTS

This treasure chest of *JEWels* would never have been discovered, polished, or shared without the jewelers who helped inspire the poems in this book and shape them until they glistened. Among the first was my friend, folklorist Ilana Harlow, who, in an offhand moment, suggested I call the inchoate work I was pondering *JEWels*.

Like prospecting and panning for gold, the process of writing this book has been an expedition, beginning with a poem-joke about a parrot that my friend Zev Shanken sent around to Brevitas, an online poetry collective dedicated to the short poem. It came together over dinners with my dear friends Flash Rosenberg and Esther Cohen, when the idea for this book was just a gleam in my eye. Esther introduced me to my agent, Susan Cohen at Writers House, who thought she would take a quick glance at the material to appease Esther, then thankfully perceived some gold veins in the ore.

Rabbi Barry Schwartz, director of The Jewish Publication Society (JPS), was next to see a glimmer of value in the poems. He suggested that commentaries and careful attention to sources were needed. My friend for the ages Marc Kaminsky sat with me, working tirelessly to edit many of the poems, wielding a pencil the way a jeweler might hold miniature pliers.

Then Joy Weinberg, JPS's managing editor, took the uncut stone and diligently and brilliantly edited the work to rise to what JPS calls, appropriately, its "gold standard." My wonderful friend, colleague, and editor Caitlin Van Dusen polished the gems and their settings. Thanks as well to the University of Nebraska Press for co-publishing this volume with JPS. Appreciation also goes to the fine editors at the University of Nebraska Press, Ann F. Baker and Virginia Perrin.

If stories were indeed jewels, Peninnah Schram would be among the world's richest people. After knowing each other for close to fifty years, we finally managed to find a way to work together. As the book's lead commentator, she not only shared her wealth of stories and storytelling knowledge, infusing the commentaries with her thoughtfulness and humor, but also contributed many JEWels herself.

There are still more jewelers to thank. Howard Schwartz's many books, particularly *Tree of Souls: Jewish Mythology*, inspired a number of these poems and provided the background for others. My friends Rose Reissman, an educator, and Bob Holman, a wonderful poet, encouraged me from the start. The editor and lifelong friend Martha Dahlen suggested the chapter on Jewish foods and masterfully edited a few of the poems. Thanks are due as well to the staff and board of City Lore, the organization I founded and direct on New York's Lower East Side, for supporting me on this seven-year journey.

The laughter (or lack thereof) of my children, Ben and Eliza, let me know which jokes were, in fact, gems. My beautiful wife, Amanda, reads everything I write—a task I would certainly not wish upon any other human being. To my brothers, Murray and Bill, my family, and the family of contributors who shared their soulful creativity for this book: you are more precious to me than any jewel.

INTRODUCTION

The Ancient Living Tradition of Jewish Jokes and Stories

Join us as we enter the cave of Jewish storytelling, hold up a miner's lamp, chip away at the schist, and sift through the dust of legends, tales, poems, jokes, and stories to find those that stand the test of time. Mining for meaning, we journey through this grotto of jokes and tales on a quest to uncover the JEWels. Then we polish them hard, so each of us can see our own reflection.

In ancient times, a chain of tales, or *chain midrashim*, inspired by the Torah, spoke of a sacred jewel called the *Tzohar*. This jewel originated in the light that illuminated the Garden of Eden with a luminosity like no other light. When Adam and Eve ate the forbidden fruit, the Garden was plunged into darkness . . . but God preserved a portion of that brilliant light in the *Tzohar*, which the angel Raziel delivered to Adam and Eve when they were expelled from the Garden. Adam gave the jewel to his son Seth, who in turn passed it on to the righteous Enoch; from there it passed to Enoch's son Methuselah, and to his son Lamech, and to his son Noah. God commanded Noah to place the *Tzohar* in the ark to illuminate his journey.

When Noah landed on Mount Ararat, he got drunk in celebration, and the gem fell from its hook on the ark and settled in an underwater cave—the very cave where, centuries later, Abraham was born. Abraham wore the sacred jewel all the days of his life. He passed it on to Isaac, who gave it to Jacob, who was wearing the stone when he dreamed of the ladder to heaven. He, in turn, willed it to Joseph, who wore it around his neck atop his coat of many colors. He wore it when he was stripped of his coat and thrown into the pit of snakes. The jewel was placed inside Joseph's coffin, and when Moses recovered his coffin years later, God told him to hang it in the tabernacle, where it was known as the *ner tamid*, the eternal light.[1] To this day, it burns above the ark in every synagogue. It is even said that light from the *Tzohar* found its way into the big fish that Jonah found himself in, and allowed him to see in the dark.

The word *Tzohar* is suggestive of the word *Zohar*, the title of the key text of kabbalistic mysticism, meaning "splendor" or "illumination."[2] The story cycle of the *Tzohar* suggests the preservation of the primordial light in a jewel. In shaping these stories and jokes into poems, I hope to bring out some tiny portion of the *Tzohar*'s leftover light, which shines forth from these compacted lines I've called JEWels.

HOW I CAME TO WRITE THIS BOOK

My own exploration of JEWels began a few years ago, when the poet and teacher Zev Shanken, part of the Brevitas online poetry collective, sent around an old Jewish joke about a parrot, written in the form of a brief poem:

> As a surprise gift for her birthday, a guy sends
> his polyglot immigrant grandmother
> a bird that speaks ten languages.
>
> A week later, he calls her up.
> *So, Grandma, how'd you like the bird?*
> *Delicious.*
>
> A second punch line:
> *What? You ate the bird? Grandma,*
> *that bird spoke ten languages!*
> *Really? So maybe he shoulda said something.*

When I first read it, I realized how well this joke worked as a poem, especially with the line breaks, which give it poetic shape on the page.

Over the years I had written several poems based on jokes from the Jewish tradition. Philosophical Jewish jokes, I discovered, lend themselves to short poetry just as well.

Likewise do great stories from the Jewish tradition. A few years ago, Rabbi Edward Schecter, known as the Storytelling Rabbi, told a simple tale in his Yom Kippur sermon at Temple Beth Shalom in Hastings-on-Hudson, New York, my hometown. He told us of the first lines of the Talmud, which ask: "From when may we recite the *Shema*, the morning prayer?" Although he spoke in prose, I heard his words as poetry, and when I got home, I set down these lines:

> The rabbis argued: *How do we know*
> *the instant night turns into day*
> *and it's time to say the morning prayer?*

The first said, *When you can tell a black thread*
from a blue.

The second, *No, when you can tell a blue thread*
from a purple.

The third, *When you can recognize the face*
of your fellow human being.

"There never was a story without a poem," writes the anthropologist Harold
Scheub in *The Poem in the Story: Music, Poetry and Narrative.* "It is in the nature
of storytelling that the narrative is constructed around a poetic interior. . . . Story
is composed of words, of images, of feelings, of rhythm: all of these conspire
to create the metaphorical yeastiness that is the poem in the story."[3] And so
began the undertaking of a lifelong dream: to combine my interest in Jewish
storytelling and humor with my passion for short poems.

ABOUT THIS BOOK

JEwels is the first book to transform the living tradition of Jewish stories and
jokes into short, accessible poems, recording and reflecting on Jewish experi-
ence from the past through to the present day, with original commentary as
well. It's a new hybrid—not a book of Jewish jokes or of Jewish stories (for each
of these genres, books abound). I boil down the jokes and stories I have been
collecting for decades to their essence—like a cook using a balsamic reduction
to reveal the flavor in a sauce.

JEwels also preserves a *living* tradition of poems, stories, and jokes, in contrast
to many earlier collections of Jewish stories that record stories and poems no
longer told. The pieces are in the tradition of found poems—in this case, found
within jokes and stories. Some might call them prose poems; others, miniatur-
ized stories in which the compressed narrative teases out the poetry within.

Jewish comedians (Lenny Bruce, Jackie Mason) appear in these pages, along-
side writers and musicians (Elie Wiesel, Sholem Aleichem, I. L. Peretz, Itzhak
Perlman) and Hasidic rabbis (the Baal Shem Tov, Rabbi Nachman of Breslov)—
yet most of the tellers are just ordinary Jews. The tales themselves come with
a cast of characters: the schlemiel (the one who spills the soup), the shlimazl
(the one it lands on), the schlepper (poor soul reduced to dragging and hauling

stuff), the schmendrick (fool), the snook (even bigger fool), the shnorrer (beggar), the shlub (unkept, slovenly sort), the nudnik (pest), the nudge (a pushier pest), the kibitzer (chatterer), the maven (big shot or expert), and the mensch (person of integrity and honor), among others. They are, in a sense, *mishpucha* (family), and perhaps there is a touch of each of them in every Jew—or perhaps in every human being.

I like to think of the poems as Jewish versions of Zen koans, the aphorisms Buddhist practitioners use during meditation to help unravel truths about the world, and themselves. These talmudic koans (not Cohens!) wend through the pageants and plagues that make up Jewish lives, helping us, I hope, to reflect on these events from a place of higher ground. And more: from this plateau, each of us may also gaze down at many of our human endeavors, as well as our own conversations and jokes, and perceive the poetry within them. I call this "the poetry of everyday life."

The sources for the poetry of everyday life are varied:

- Jewish jokes with philosophical overtones or poetic punch lines ("Rich Man," "Taxi")
- Jewish jokes that rise to the level of poetry because of the inflections and rhythms of a particular teller ("Passementerie")
- Jewish jokes to which the writer added a twist to amplify their humor and meaning ("Einstein's Theory of Relativity," "My Mother Liked Telling Jokes")
- brief philosophical stories from the Jewish tradition that have the quality of adages, some of which helped inspire this book ("The Beautiful Question," "Concerto")
- folktales from the Hasidic tradition ("Levi Yitzhak Burns the Evidence")
- poems that tell Jewish stories or embody talmudic thinking ("The Sabbath Fish," "The Razbash on Old Age")
- original poems that emerge from a Jewish or talmudic sensibility ("Rachel," "A Rabbinical Love Poem")
- prose passages in which a poem is hidden ("Stories," "The Laughing Man")
- snatches of Jewish mythology ("Soul Sight," "The Angel of Death")
- overheard conversations among Jews ("The DNA in My Coffee")

Some of these pieces may simply make you laugh. Others exist in that profound and nebulous human space where one does not know whether to laugh or cry. After all, Jewish humor, the writers William Novak and Moshe Waldoks suggest, "is a kind of verbal equivalent to the blues."[4] The writer Irving Kristol described it as a "a victory gained by the Jewish spirit over centuries of adversity, an exultant defiance of persecution and harassment, an affirmation of the will to survival in the face of an ever impending doom."[5] As a storyteller quipped at one of my lectures, "Jewish people always wanted to laugh at situations, even at times when they should have cried."

In chapter 6, Zev Shanken retells this contemporary joke that lands betwixt the genres with a thud: a powerful poem about the Holocaust, disguised as a joke.

> A comedian dies and goes to heaven.
> He meets God and says,
> *Are you okay with Holocaust jokes?*
>
> God says, *Try me.*
> The comedian tells God the joke.
> God says, *I don't get it.*
>
> The comedian replies,
> *Well, I guess you had to be there.*

When I felt there was much more to say about a piece, I explored and expressed salient ideas by presenting accompanying commentary, set to some extent in the style of commentary one finds in the Talmud. As such I hope to suggest the talmudic quality of Jewish storytelling—in this case with the select poems prompting related ideas and sometimes even reinterpretation. Like the Talmud, which Jews have pored over (also read: argue over) for generations, Jewish storytelling and joke-telling is a living tradition of ongoing dialogue. In effect, you the reader become part of the conversation with the poets and commentators in this book.

The lead commentator for these poems is Peninnah Schram, the doyenne of Jewish storytelling and winner of the National Jewish Book Award as well as the Covenant Foundation Award for Outstanding Jewish Educator. Among the other poets and storytellers I've drawn upon for comments (and whom you can learn more about in the Commentator Biographies) are five collaborators who have helped shape this book from the beginning: Rabbi Edward Schecter; humorist and former cartoon editor for the *New Yorker* Bob Mankoff; monologist and

Moth storyteller Flash Rosenberg; poet and activist Esther Cohen; and poet and teacher Zev Shanken, who often presents his commentaries and poems in the name of The Razbash, a fictitious rabbi representing his wiser self:

> The Razbash is an acronym
> for Rabbi Zev ben Shlomo,
> my nom de plume if I were
> a medieval rabbi of note.
>
> *R* stands for rabbi,
> *ben* is Hebrew for "son of," and
> Shlomo is my father's Hebrew name.
>
> I invented him to do the Jewish work
> I was too busy teaching
> and writing poetry to do.
>
> But after a while I discovered
> that he, too, was a poet and teacher,
> and had a better understanding
> of Judaism, humor, and people than I.
>
> So now I let him do his own thing
> and I just drop in from time to time
> to see if he needs anything.[6]

To me, the essence of this work is best articulated by one of my collaborators, the poet Marc Kaminsky:

> Cultural and mystical meanings, the sacred and the transgressive, collide. Some are self-deprecating and materialistic; others are talmudic and spiritual. Some offer wonderment and speculation. Some open up the world; some provide closure. Some exude that surplus of meanings that can incite a reverie; others just close with a punch line. Some suggest the perplexity of living, others a burst of sexual and appetitive energy— the light from on high, the fart from below. They range from Hasidic mysticism to Jewish sarcasm. Some exhale the meaning of what can't be said. Some overturn the order of everyday life; others hint at the essence of God.

The nearly 180 poems in *JEWels* are mined from the quarries of poetic material found during different times and different experiences of Jews in history. I have found JEWels "In Stories" (chapter 1); "On a Journey," including pilgrimages (chapter 2); "From the Old Country" (chapter 3); "In Jokes" (chapter 4); in passages inspired by or "From Torah" (chapter 5); in stories "Shaped by the Holocaust" (chapter 6); "In Glimpses of Jewish American Lives" (chapter 7); "In Jewish Foods" (chapter 8); "In Conversations with God" (chapter 9); and in humorous and profound ideas "On the Meaning of Life" (chapter 10).

As such, the genesis of each poem varies. Some have always been poems or have been excerpted or adapted from original poems for this book. Others are traditional or contemporary Jewish jokes or tales now rendered as poems. Still others have been lined out or newly adapted from oral or written narratives into poems—often, but not always, by me. To clarify all this for readers and scholars, each poem is followed by an attribution. Some attributions are simply labeled "traditional joke" or "traditional tale." If the poem was originally a poem, the attribution reads "by" the name of the poet. When another author or I transformed an oral or written narrative into a poem, the attribution reads: "adapted by," followed by the name of the adapter and the title of the work. Whenever I lined out a passage of prose into a poem without any adaptations, the attribution reads: "lined out from" the title of the original work (I am not mentioned). Whenever I could recall who relayed the joke or story to me, the label reads "retold by." Whenever possible, more information about the underlying works appears in the Notes. Usually, poems that are not annotated are original to this volume.

"Final Thoughts" reflects on the portability of Jewish humor and storytelling; and the "Questions for Discussion" (about seven thought questions for each chapter) should help facilitate using *JEWels* in Jewish book groups, university courses, adult education, and other settings. And as noted, "Commentator Biographies" introduce the various commentators whose observations are integral to this volume.

Inasmuch as this collection covers a wide swath of Jewish experience, it also contains certain biases on the part of this author. The terrain is, broadly speaking, the topics in Jewish history and life that have intrigued and inspired me. The issues explored in the poems tend to be close to my own lived experience as an American Jewish man of Ashkenazi Jewish heritage whose mother's family immigrated from the town of Shpola, near the banks of the River Khovkivka in Ukraine between 1905 and 1910. My Hebrew name is Shmuel (Hebrew: שמואל), a name I've used for a few appropriate characters in these poems.

Many potential subjects—including Jewish women's experiences, Israeli folklore, and Sephardic customs, among others—remain to be covered in greater depth. Also, I have not shied away from including stories and jokes about sex. The bawdy streak that runs through Jewish jokes and stories has long been relished by certain "members of the tribe," myself included.

CLOSING THOUGHTS

In the ancient commentaries, it is said that there are four types of students who sit among the Sages: the sponge, the funnel, the strainer, and the sieve. The sponge absorbs everything; the funnel lets things in from one side and lets them out the other; the strainer lets the wine flow through and retains the sediment; and the sieve allows the flour dust to pass through and retains only the fine flour.[7] For this book I stood before the Sages of Jewish humor and storytelling with a sieve, then sought to knead the flour of prose into short, accessible poems that express a range of Jewish perspectives on the human experience. I extract from and adapt the stories and jokes for their hilarious, sardonic, ironic, idiosyncratic, sometimes bitter, often tragicomic wisdom. I have internalized and then shaped them into a form that resonates with me, expresses who I am in this world, and offers me a useful take on living. My hope is that they will do the same for you. As storyteller Cherie Karo Schwartz writes,

> We tell our story
> from our Jewish soul: we read it, speak it, sign it, sing it.
> We dance it, draw it, drum it, dream it
> from our overflowing hearts
> and into the soul of the world.[8]

So let us embark on this improbable journey to discover a quarry of meaning by excavating the gems—hard truths with edges of wit and wonder found in the chinks and crags of Jewish lives.

JEWELS

1 JEWels . . . *in Stories*

"IT WAS FAMILY LIFE," MARC KAMINSKY'S GRANDMOTHER TOLD HIM. "It was *simkhes*, happy occasions and not such happy occasions, but it was always a *tish mit mentschn*." It was a table with people. "Everything I remember, the events of my life, holidays and times of grief, news from the family—all the gatherings took place here at the kitchen table."

And what did they do at that table but talk? "Talk . . . great torrents of boundless, exalted talk . . . has ever been the joy of the Jewish people," writes novelist and cultural critic Michael Gold. "Talk does not exhaust Jews as it does other people, nor give them brain fatigue; it refreshes them. Talk is the baseball, the gold, the poker, the love, and the war" of being Jewish. "Even old Mrs. Fingerman's parrot talked more than other parrots. Mr. Fingerman's last distraction before he died was to teach the parrot to curse in Yiddish."[1]

A storytelling tradition has been part of the Jewish heritage from the earliest times. Storytelling took place in the synagogue during public worship, on feast days, on the Sabbath, and on ordinary weekdays. "Ultimately," writes folklorist Barbara Kirshenblatt-Gimblett, "oral tradition is an institution in Jewish religious learning as sacred as the written word."[2]

"Why were human beings created?" goes a traditional Jewish saying I learned from the writer Elie Wiesel. "Because God loves stories."[3]

I myself like to trace the reason back to the prophet Elijah, considered the harbinger of the Messiah. Jews symbolically open the door for Elijah during the Passover seder, in a moment pregnant with the possibility of his—and, later, the Messiah's—portentous arrival. It is said that Elijah returns in every generation to knock three times on cottage doors. Perhaps that's because he knows "three knocks" is the way many Jewish stories begin . . . and he returns in each generation to make sure these stories are still told and handed down. Because God loves stories.[4]

"What remains of a story after it is finished?" asks Elie Wiesel, who then answers, "Another story."[5] This book of the poetry in Jewish storytelling begins with a series of poems about stories.

COMMENTARY: This tale is based on a Hasidic story about the founder of Hasidism, Rabbi Israel ben Eliezer (1700–1760), also known as the Baal Shem Tov (Master of the Good Name). Many Jewish writers have retold the tale, including Gershom Scholem, Martin Buber, and Elie Wiesel, the latter in his classic book *The Gates of the Forest*.[6]

I open the book with this story because I believe that if ever the day comes when Jewish culture is truly endangered, its stories and humor—imbued with so much poetry—will, in their telling, provide the breath that can rekindle the fire, which will recall the prayer and light our way back to the place in the forest where Jewish tradition resonates within each of us. (Steve Zeitlin)

Now the Story

ADAPTED BY STEVE ZEITLIN FROM A TALE BY RABBI NACHMAN OF BRESLOV

When the great Hasid, the Baal Shem Tov
wrestled with a problem
he would seek refuge in a certain part of the forest,
light a fire, say a prayer,
and receive wisdom.

Later, a son of one of his disciples
in the same predicament,
went to the same place.
But, having arrived, could not recall the prayer,
failed to rekindle the fire.

Nevertheless, he asked for wisdom . . .
and it was sufficient.

Today, Rabbi Ben Kurzer sits in his study
with his head in his hands
Lord of All That Is, look, now.
We have forgotten the prayer,
We cannot kindle a fire,
We cannot find the place in the forest.
All we know is the story of how it was done.
Now, Lord, that, too, must be sufficient.

And it was.

Stories

ADAPTED BY STEVE ZEITLIN FROM A STORY BY GERMAN
JEWISH WRITER EDGAR HILSENRATH[7]

A Rabbi listens to the wind
as it rushes past the window of a train.

He nods his head.
Yes, it's true, the Nazis were fools.

They plundered our houses,
dug up our gardens,
shuttered our accounts—
but left our valuables untouched.

The wind protests—
But they have taken everything of value!

Except, the Rabbi says, *the most precious—*
our stories.
We brought them with us.

COMMENTARY: This midrashic tale reflects the history of the Jewish people speaking of loss. Yet what has never been fully lost, stolen, or destroyed is learning—the wealth of stories, sacred and secular, that continue to be held as Jewish treasures. This message has been transmitted from generation to generation in many versions. Like the wind personified in this poem, Jews are a people who travel (not always by choice) and have lived in almost every corner of the world. What's lighter to carry than stories in the heart? (Peninnah Schram)

Along with the light and portable stories, many Jews bore the crushing weight of the Holocaust. Edgar Hilsenrath, who inspired this poem, was a Holocaust survivor. When millions of Jews lost their lives in the camps, they lost not only the stories they remembered but also the unfolding stories of their lives. (Steve Zeitlin)

Tales

LINED OUT FROM AN INSCRIPTION IN ELIE WIESEL'S *SOULS ON FIRE*[8]

My father, an enlightened spirit, believed in man.
My grandfather, a fervent Hasid, believed in God.
The one taught me to speak, the other to sing.
Both loved stories.

COMMENTARY: This poem brings to mind my own parents, both immigrants to the United States: my father from Lithuania in 1906, my mother from Belarus in 1926. They told me very different kinds of stories. My mother would tell a specific didactic tale to teach me to restrain my temper. Once, when I didn't want to hear it, I called out, "Ma, I don't want to hear that story again! I've heard it a hundred times!" What did my mother answer? "You'll hear it a hundred and one times!" Yes, I told that same story to my children, many times, when they were growing up. My father told biblical and talmudic tales, mostly. The earliest remembered story that I loved and asked him to tell me again and again was about the prophet Elijah. He also sang folksongs to me, including a lullaby his mother used to sing to him in Lithuania. We often sang it as a duet. From my mother's personal stories of pogroms and teaching tales, I learned how to behave and be a Jew. My father opened the path to wonder and curiosity through his stories and songs. I became a storyteller thanks to both my parents. (Peninnah Schram)

The Lubavitcher Rebbe on Stories

BY ESTHER COHEN

Years ago,
when my brother's friend Linda
worked for the *New York Times Magazine*,
I pitched her a piece about the Lubavitcher Rebbe
in Crown Heights.

Yes.

My childhood friend Abby, a photographer now,
came too. She took pictures, I asked questions.
We went many times.

The Lubavitcher Rebbe was nothing like
anyone else. He sat in a dark room
with black books on shelves. He was wearing
his Lubavitcher Rebbe outfit.

Many people would come and ask him "What should I do?" questions.
Sometimes he'd let me listen.

How many questions are there? I asked him.
How many stories do people tell?

Seventy-two, he said. *There are seventy-two
stories. Listen carefully. You will hear them all.*

COMMENTARY: In Jewish mystical practice there are seventy-two names of God. Taken from the Jewish mystics' observation that in the book of Exodus, each of three consecutive verses (14:19–21) that describe three divine attributes contains seventy-two letters, seventy-two has become the proverbial number of stories and questions in all of life. That might be just what the Lubavitcher Rebbe had in mind. (Peninnah Schram)

Burning the Scrolls

ADAPTED BY STEVE ZEITLIN FROM A TALE RETOLD
BY RABBI EDWARD SCHECTER[9]

In a midrash from the time of the Romans,
Titus' men set Torah scrolls
ablaze in the town square.

The other Rabbis stood aghast.
Why do you weep?
a student asked.

See! The parchment burns, he continued,
yet the letters ascend upward through the heavens.

When we tell our stories
we bring the letters
back onto the parchment,

for our lives are like tales
told
between the lines of ancient scrolls.

COMMENTARY: In the Zohar (radiance), the foundational work of Kabbalah, it is written that the Torah is "black fire on white fire." What seems to be black ink on white parchment is in fact black fire on white fire. Some believe that the black refers to the fiery letters and the white to the spaces between them. Others hold that the letters are black fire set against the white fire of God's creation. (Rabbi Edward Schecter)

Rabbi Avi Weiss offers a different interpretation: The black letters represent the cognitive message, while the white spaces represent that which goes beyond the world of the intellect. "The black letters are limited," he writes, "limiting, and fixed. The white spaces, on the other hand, catapult us into the realm of the limitless and the ever-changing, ever-growing. They are the silence, the song, the story."[10] (Peninnah Schram)

A Table with People

BY POET AND THERAPIST MARC KAMINSKY[11]

You said: Thirty years ago
I had my brothers and little kids
and it was family life
It was happy occasions and not such happy occasions,
but it was always *a tish mit mentshn.*

Stories of the good times
and the bad
came back to you, happenings
you had gone over
countless times, repeating life
in the imagination.

Oh Bubba, at your table
I entered your stories
as they entered me,
thinking: all those lives
that have passed
into your own
they go on
speaking through you,
and I will continue them.

And I felt this terrific enlargement
as your memories became
my memories.

Now I wonder: How much, after
all, can be carried on? What
will die with you
when you die? What
pitiable or perishable thing
will the world lose?

The shtetl of Kostuchohn?
The way you saw the gentleman
of the geese watching
over the little ones
in your grandmother's yard?
The smell of the embroidered tablecloth
in your linen closet?

COMMENTARY: I have loved Marc Kaminsky's poem from the time I first read it. The imagery of a *tish mit mentshn*, "a table with people," brings to mind the huge oak table that dominated my parents' dining room. It was always covered by layers of tablecloths. And in between those tablecloths my mother would keep her bills, receipts, pieces of paper with messages written to herself, photos, and articles she cut from the Yiddish newspaper, these mainly containing advice for young women that she would pass on to me.

The table was my mother's soft-sculpture filing cabinet. Yet when a friend would stop by, instantly a cup of tea, a glass dish filled with homemade cherry jelly, and a honey cake would appear on the table. I used to wonder how everything stayed in place even on the utilitarian table. And then on Shabbat or a *yom tov* (Jewish holiday), a beautiful white lace tablecloth would cover it, along with the good china, silverware, and *Kiddush* cups. Magically, the room was transformed, the family (mostly) would gather around it, and it truly became a table with people, crowned with a cornucopia of stories. (Peninnah Schram)

JEWELS . . . *on a Journey*

THE JEWS FLED EGYPT WITHOUT ENOUGH TIME TO ALLOW THEIR BREAD to rise. Jews have always been a "portable people," traveling from place to place—sometimes directed by God, other times by humans; sometimes escaping from dire straits, other times seeking a better life.

In biblical times, these portable people followed the Torah's commandment to make a pilgrimage on foot to the Jerusalem Temple three times a year. At the time of the First Temple (1200–586 BCE) and then the Second Temple (586 BCE–70 CE), the Jews brought sacrifices in celebration of three holidays known as *Shalosh Regalim*—now the holidays of Passover, Shavuot, and Sukkot. It was an arduous journey in those times, but many thousands would ascend to Jerusalem—a topographical and spiritual ascent.

The Jewish people's journey motif begins with Abraham. God tells him: "Go forth from your native land and from your father's house to a land that I will show you" (Gen. 12:1). Author David Arnow characterizes it as a journey of hope: "Abraham packs up his wife, a nephew, and all the wealth they had amassed and 'went forth as YHWH [God] had commanded him' [Gen. 12:4]. On the surface the trial would seem to involve Abraham's accepting God's commandment to abandon a familiar place, leave his aged father, and set off for an undefined destination. Yet in my view God's command reached even deeper. It tested the strength of the two core qualities of hope itself—the willingness to embrace the possibility of a future fundamentally different than the present and the readiness to help bring it about."[1]

In the years that followed, as the Jews traveled, they often did so without luggage. But they always took a form of Torah with them—that is, Jewish learning transmitted from generation to generation. That learning embodied their hope. When Peninnah Schram's parents made the fear-filled but courageous decision to leave their home in Eastern Europe for America, both carried what she calls "Bundles of Rainbows"—bundles of hope.

These are poems about Jews on their journeys.

COMMENTARY: This Chelm (or Helm) tale, about the legendary town of fools, is told in many versions, including those by the storyteller Steven Sanfield. In one of the humorous versions, Pinya the Chelmite is on his way to Warsaw, and one night before sleeping he places his shoes pointing toward the big city. However, unbeknownst to him, a stranger turns his shoes around. In the morning, he follows the direction in which the shoes point. At the end of the story, he realizes he has "returned" to Chelm because "there can't be two wives such as mine!"[3] (Peninnah Schram)

In one of his lectures at New York City's 92nd Street Y, Elie Wiesel told another version of this story, comparing the Chelmite to the German and Polish Jewish families who returned to their hometowns after the war, looked in the windows of their former homes, now inhabited by other families, and felt a bit like the man whose shoes were turned around. Wiesel also spoke of returning to his former home in Sighet, Romania, after the war, in the dark, and digging up a watch, given to him as a bar mitzvah present, that he had buried in the backyard. He started walking away, then felt guilty and started running, clasping the dirt-covered watch in his hand. Suddenly he felt like a thief and rushed back to rebury it, promising never to return again. (Rabbi Edward Schecter)

Rabbi Lawrence Kushner writes that "Judaism has many legends of people who go on spiritual journeys. The searcher who has just arrived is rewarded with the final question 'And now that you have survived and beheld these wonders, do you choose to remain here with "us" or will you return to your spouse and children?'"[4] In a general sense, this question confronts us all. Do we say to ourselves, "Goodness, I forgot all about the people I love and need to get back right away"? Or do we begin anew? (Steve Zeitlin)

Paradise

ADAPTED BY STEVE ZEITLIN FROM A TRADITIONAL
TALE RETOLD BY RABBI EDWARD SCHECTER[2]

Shmuel awakens, determined to find
the fabled town of Paradise.

He doesn't realize his children have followed him.

He travels deep into the night
till he finds himself, drained and weary, on a mountainside.

Before sleep,
he takes off his shoes and points the toes toward Paradise
to remember the direction the next morning.

While he's sleeping,
some say a spirit—others say his children—
turns his shoes around.

Waking, he proceeds in the direction of his shoes.
Discovers a house that looks just like his house,
children who look just like his children,
a woman who looks just like his wife.

Convinced he's now in Paradise,
some say he moves in—
and finds an oh-so-much-better life.

Others say he exclaims, *Oh dear!*
Every place is the same!
So I may as well stay here.

COMMENTARY: Jews have often sought spiritual homes outside the borders of their own religion, not only as practitioners but as leaders. In her book *American JewBu*, sociologist Emily Sigalow notes American Jews' significant role in the popularization of meditation and mindfulness in the United States.[5] Pilgrimage stories and jokes like this one have been told ever since Jews started becoming gurus! Another joke compares the questions of a Buddhist and a Jew. The Buddhist asks, "What is the sound of one hand clapping?" The Jew asks, "If a Jewish husband is alone in a forest, and he says something and his wife doesn't hear it, is he still wrong?" (Steve Zeitlin)

The Guru

CONTEMPORARY JOKE RETOLD BY STEVE ZEITLIN

A woman awakens one morning
with an uncontrollable urge to visit a guru in the Himalayas.

She purchases a ticket, flies to Kathmandu,

hires a car,
a team of donkeys,
and a Sherpa
to guide her to his temple.

She knocks on the door,
asks a monk to see the famous guru.

He has no time for anyone except the Buddhist holy men,
the monk replies.

She pitches a tent outside the temple,
stays for seven nights and seven days,
knocks upon the door seven times each day.

Finally, the monk comes to the door.

Enough—he will see you,
alone, briefly, under one condition:
you will be limited to three words.

She agrees,
is let into the temple alone.

When the door swings open,
she says these words:
Sheldon, come home.

COMMENTARY: Throughout the ages, wherever Jews lived, they created a Jewish vernacular that integrated the languages of the surrounding countries and, always, Hebrew. When they lived in Germany, their vernacular was a conglomeration of medieval German, Slavic languages, French, and Hebrew.

The word *mensch* means "person" in German, but in Yiddish it takes on the added meaning of what kind of person you are—a "good person." Essentially, *mensch* reflects estimations of one's character, values, and ethical behavior. My mother used to say, "A mensch is a mensch." With this marvelous word, one doesn't have to qualify it in any way. Who needs to say, "You are a good mensch," "You are a thoughtful mensch," "You are a generous mensch." A mensch is a mensch! (Peninnah Schram)

Mameloshen

BY STEVE ZEITLIN

Shmuel searched for the lost land of Yiddish
in a few words his grandmother Bella
didn't want him to understand.

Too old to learn the language,
he ransacked the punch lines.

There he found *mameloshen*—the mother tongue.

And so he went on
to explore tastes—
cholent, knishes, blintzes,
Aunt Mitzi's *matzah brei*,
bagels with a schmear of cream cheese.

And then the discovery:
mamaliga comes from the Romanians,
borscht from the Russians,
falafel from the Palestinians,
cholent from the Poles.

So he searched for his homeland, adrift in words,

like a lost mammal asking what it means to be human,
or a troubled child seeking grandma's advice.
You must always be a decent person, she began,
a good, kind person, a . . .

Then she kneaded all of *mameloshen*
into a single word—
mensch.

COMMENTARY: The Razbash (my fictitious rabbi) says the word *once* should appear at the end of Bubba Truth's message, so it reads, "Tell them I was young and beautiful once." This way, they will understand that life is fleeting and must not be wasted. (Zev Shanken)

Bubba Truth

ADAPTED BY STEVE ZEITLIN FROM A TRADITIONAL TALE RETOLD
BY WRITER AND FOLKTALE COLLECTOR JANE YOLEN[6]

Shmuel awoke one morning
with an urge to search
for Truth. He set forth, traveling

up mountains, down valleys,
across rivers, through villages, cities, and towns,
through wetlands and wastelands

and fields of wildflowers in bloom.

He searched until days turned
to weeks, months, years.

One day, as he scaled a cliff,
he found an age-old, wizened woman
in an unmarked cave, her face

wrinkled as a walnut,
a snaggletooth mouth,
her voice lyrical and low.

She beckoned to him
with a wave of her weathered hand.

He called her Grandmother—Bubba Truth,
studied with her for a year and a day, amazed
by her deep knowledge, the wisdom of her ways.

When Shmuel had learned all he could,
he stood at the entrance to the cave.
I've come to bid you farewell, he said.
My mind and heart are full.

But before I go, Bubba Truth, tell me,
is there any message you want me to bring
to the yearning peoples of the world?

Yes, she said. *Tell them I was young and beautiful.*

Traveler's Prayer

BY RABBI SHEILA PELTZ WEINBERG[7]

A prayer for the journey.
We could say it every day
When we first leave the soft warmth of our beds
And don't know for sure if we'll return at night,
When we get into the trains, planes and automobiles
And put our lives into the hands of strangers,
Or when we leave our homes for a day, a week, a month or more—
Will we return home to a peaceful home? Untouched by fire, flood or
   crime?
How will our travels change us?
What gives us the courage to go through the door?

A prayer for the journey,
For the journey we take in this fragile vessel of flesh,
A finite number of years and we will reach
The unknown, where it all began.
Every life, every day, every hour is a journey.
In the travel is the discovery.
The wisdom, the joy.
Every life, every day, every hour is a journey.
In the travel is the reward,
The peace, the blessing.

3 ✦ JEWels . . . *from the Old Country*

"[The shtetl was] a jumble of wooden houses clustered higgledy-piggledy about a marketplace," writes Maurice Samuel, "the streets . . . as tortuous as a Talmudic argument . . . bent into question marks and folded into parentheses."[1] The Holocaust obliterated the Jewish shtetl and enshrined it in memory. The stage musical and film *Fiddler on the Roof* (based on Yiddish writer Sholem Aleichem's Tevye the Milkman stories), Marc Chagall's paintings, and some influential books about the shtetl (Marc Zborowski and Elizabeth Herzog's *Life Is with People*, Maurice Samuel's *The World of Sholom Aleichem*, and Bella Chagall's *Burning Lights*, among others) imbued the small Jewish towns with a nostalgic glow. The shtetl Jews "were the real Jews," Rabbi Edward Schecter told his Reform congregation, "and we [see ourselves as] a poor facsimile, ashamed that we don't know what they know, don't observe what they observe, don't spend as much time being Jewish as they do."[2]

Yet such imagery of the shtetl oversimplifies the complexities of Jewish life and history in Eastern Europe. Barbara Kirshenblatt-Gimblett notes that in English the term *shtetl* tends to conjure an imagined community, whereas in Yiddish *shtetl* is often just a word for "town."[3]

In this book, the shtetl serves as a locus for stories. Even though the Pale of Settlement in Eastern Europe encompassed cities, towns, and villages, American storytellers have routinely set their tales in the village shtetls. And though only a few Jewish jokes are still set in Eastern Europe—most have gradually migrated to American settings—many favorite Jewish folktales told by American-born tellers are still set in an old country imagined by those without any firsthand knowledge of that place and time.

Fascination about and nostalgia for the partially imagined shtetl—still in the memories of some elder Jews and present in the stories they pass on to their children—have assured it a firm place in Jewish American folklore, regardless of the stories' historical accuracy. In a world forever changed by the Holocaust, stories about the shtetl are a way of saying *Kaddish* (the mourner's prayer) for an obliterated way of life.

COMMENTARY: In the 1500s, the kabbalist and mystic Rabbi Yosef Karo authored the *Shulchan Arukh*, the code of Jewish law. He believed that his *maggid* (preacher) leaned over his shoulder and whispered stories into his ear. Five hundred years later, Cherie Karo Schwartz, who carries the Karo family name through her father, firmly believes she is related to the famous rabbi, who now leans over her shoulder and whispers stories into her ear. (Her London-born maternal bubbe, Rae Olesh, also a storyteller, whispers family tales into her other ear.) My rendering is inspired by her fish tale, a variant of both the classic Eastern European folktale "Yosef Who Loved Shabbat" and the Israel Folktale Archives' Yemenite version, which are themselves based on an ancient Babylonian Talmud tale about the wonders of keeping the Sabbath. (Steve Zeitlin)

The Sabbath Fish

ADAPTED BY STEVE ZEITLIN FROM CHERIE KARO SCHWARTZ'S
VERSION OF JEWISH FOLKLORE FROM EASTERN EUROPE AND
YEMEN, AND EARLIER FROM THE BABYLONIAN TALMUD[4]

The Jews keep the Sabbath
and the Sabbath keeps the Jews.

So Jacob the jeweler shuts his store,
even though the golden ring
the crooked rich man brought him to repair
is missing from his drawer,
even though the crooked rich man likely stole it back,
disposed of the ring beneath the ground or in the sea,
so that Jacob will owe him all he owns.

The Sabbath!
Jacob sends his daughter to the market
for a fresh-caught Sabbath fish.

She sets it on their dinner platter.

He is carving it from head to tail
when a glint of gold shines through the scales.

Merit of the Sabbath, he declares.

COMMENTARY: There is a fine line between magic and miracles. In biblical times, Jews were skeptical of magic. Deuteronomy 18:10–11 states that a Jew is forbidden from being a "soothsayer, or an augur, or a sorcerer, or a charmer, or a medium, or a wizard, or a necromancer." Often, Jews suggest that magic exists for others but not for them. One's own experiences are considered miracles, whereas other people's are deemed the result of tricks, superstitions, or magic. God's presence and intervention in this story suggest that what happens here is not magic but a miracle. In the story about the Golem that follows, the reader can decide: magic or miracle? (Steve Zeitlin)

The Magic Ship

ADAPTED BY STEVE ZEITLIN FROM FOLKLORIST AND AUTHOR HOWARD SCHWARTZ'S TELLING OF A FOLKTALE IN THE ISRAEL FOLKTALE ARCHIVES[5]

During the Spanish Inquisition,
Rabbi Shimon ben Tsemah Duran
was imprisoned with three other men
on the island of Majorca.

Three days before their execution,
the Rabbi began to draw on the wall.
The three men watched, amazed.
First he drew the vessel,
then likenesses of each of the three men
aboard the ship.

On execution day,
as the lock on the prison cell turned,
the Rabbi called out the secret, sacred name of G-d!
At once, the four men were on that boat, gliding on the high seas,
sailing toward a port in North Africa.

COMMENTARY: This story within a story is drawn from a teaching in *Sefer ha-Emunah*, a thirteenth-century kabbalistic text about the lost twenty-third letter of the Hebrew alphabet. To the kabbalists, finding that lost letter was a way to bring wholeness to the world.[6]

The classic story of the Golem of Prague tells that Rabbi Judah Loew built the gargantuan creature in the sixteenth century to respond to a charge of blood libel, the despicable falsehood that Jews were killing Christian children to use their blood in satanic rituals. In an earlier version of the story, "The Golem of Rabbi Elijah," also retold by folktale collector Jacob Grimm in the nineteenth century, Rabbi Elijah, seeking protection for the Jews, fashions the Frankenstein-like figure by writing the word *emet* (truth) on his forehead and reciting G-d's sacred name. When the Golem grows too powerful and needs to be stopped, Rabbi Elijah takes away the *e* in *emet* so that it spells *met* (dead), and the creature collapses.[7]

The poem, built on foundations of mysteries, on worlds beyond the world we know, speaks to the power of individual letters of the Hebrew alphabet, of words, and of stories in Jewish mythology and consciousness. (Steve Zeitlin)

Tales of the Razbash

BY POET AND TEACHER ZEV SHANKEN

The Hebrew alphabet has 22 letters, but it originally had 23.
Sefer ha-Emunah tells us
that if the missing letter were restored,
every defect in our present world would be repaired.

What sound did the letter make?

Some say it made the sound
of the child in a basement barrel, hiding from the Cossacks.
To be certain not to make a sound, he stuffed his throat
with rags he found in the dark.
When he tasted kerosene,
he let out a soft shriek of agony,
which the angels say
had not been heard since
the 23rd letter was lost.

Others say the sound is the unutterable name of G-d,
which the great Rabbi of Prague inscribed
on the forehead of a clay statue
to frighten antisemites.
To the Rabbi's delight and shock,
his creation, the Golem, worked too well.
Yes, the antisemites were defeated,
but so was the entire world—almost—
because the monster misunderstood his directive.
When ordered to frighten all evil antisemites,
the monster understood he was to frighten all evil—

until he heard the Rabbi say
the sound of the missing letter backward
and the Golem slowly turned back into clay.

COMMENTARY: The ancient Rabbis sat down to decide when the people should recite the evening *Shema*, the Jewish affirmation of faith. This was so important, their discussion began on the very first line of the Mishnah, the earliest record of how the Jews interpreted the Torah, passed down orally for hundreds of years before being written down (c. 200 CE). The Rabbis respond to the Mishnah in sometimes quite lengthy discussions called the Gemara. I cannot tell you the length of time of this particular discussion, but I can say it went on for about fifty pages (in the Steinsaltz edition). The Rabbis did not take the discussion lightly! (Robert J. Bernstein)

The Rabbis' Convocation

TRADITIONAL TALE RETOLD BY THERAPIST AND
WRITER ROBERT J. BERNSTEIN[8]

Three Rabbis argue over the precise time
to say the *Shema*.

The first one says it's when the Rabbis
conclude their convocation.

The second one says it's when the last sliver of sun
slips below the horizon.

The third one says it's when the tired laborer
returns home, sheds his shoes,
sits down at the table,
and sprinkles salt on his bread.

COMMENTARY: A true story: As Golda Meir was being interviewed by a journalist who was acting very obsequious, she turned to him and said, "Don't be so humble. You're not so great." (Rabbi Edward Schecter)

The Sweeper

TRADITIONAL JOKE

On Yom Kippur, the elders jockey for a front-row seat
at a synagogue in Vilna.

The rabbi speaks first.
I lead the congregation.
I know the Torah by heart.
But still I am nothing in the eyes of God.

The *macher* speaks next.
I am the richest man in the village,
but still I am nothing in the eyes of God.

Then Jakob, the lowly *shammes*, the sweeper,
stumbles to the podium.
I, too, am nothing, he says.

The *macher* whispers to the Rabbi,
Just who does he think he is?
The rabbi says,
Yeah, look who thinks he's a nothing.

THE SHAMMES: A RESPONSE

ADAPTED BY STEVE ZEITLIN FROM RABBI EDWARD SCHECTER'S
RETELLING OF "THE SWEEPER" WITH KEY YIDDISH WORDS

What's missing from this poem
is the Yiddish word *gornisht*.
In Yiddish there is the phrase *Ich bin ein Gornisht*—"I am a nothing."
Still I am a gornisht in the eyes of God.

So the shammes comes to the podium and says,
I, too, am a gornisht,
and the rabbi whispers to the *macher*,
Look who's calling himself a gornisht.

COMMENTARY: When the Rabbi of Mendov saw the glass was filled with water, not wine, he was presented with a dilemma: Should he make the blessing over wine, *boreh p'ri ha-gefen*, or should he make the blessing over water, *she-ha-kol niheyeh bi-devaro*? The choice the Rabbi made proves he was worthy of his fame. He made the blessing over wine, even though he knew it was the incorrect blessing. Why? Because he understood it is a greater sin to embarrass the poor than it is to make the wrong blessing. (Zev Shanken)

Fables often conclude with "The moral of the story is . . . ," and yet sometimes we discover that our own moral differs from what others have written. As a storyteller, I believe one of the gifts we can give ourselves—and our listeners—is to allow a story to be interpreted by each of us individually, to enrich our respective gifts of curiosity and wonder. In this story, water is symbolic of Torah and also of life. So maybe the people in the village who poured water into the barrel were sending a different but valid message. (Peninnah Schram)

Once Upon a Time in the Old Country

ADAPTED BY STEVE ZEITLIN FROM A TRADITIONAL
TALE RETOLD BY RABBI DAVID HOLTZ[9]

The famed Rabbi of Mendov
planned a visit to the village of Minsk.

In preparation, the elders agreed
to offer him a celebratory cask of wine.
He could raise a glass to mark the occasion,
and they could honor him with a special *Kiddush*.

They placed an oak barrel in the center of town.
Every Shabbes, they told the people,
bring a small pitcher of wine
and pour it into the cask.

Every week, on Shabbes, just after sundown,
Reb Schlomo whispered to his daughter: *We are not*
a rich family. Why don't we just fill our pitcher
with water? When you take it to the barrel,
pour it right at the lip. With so many
contributing, no one will notice it.

The day of the visit arrived. The Rabbi of Mendov
appeared before a cheering crowd,
accepted a beautiful *Kiddush* cup
so he could imbibe the community's blessings
and bless them in return.

He placed the cup beneath the spigot, filled it, lifted it high.
The crowd gasped. A sudden hush. It was filled to the brim
with water.

If you ever feel that that your contribution doesn't matter,
that you may let others do for you,
consider: they all may do as you would do.
If you are hesitant to march or give—to take the risk—
consider the day the revered Rabbi of Mendov
paid a visit to the village of Minsk.

COMMENTARY: This is believed to be a true story of Moses Mendelssohn and the merchant's daughter Fromet Guggenheim. The first time I heard it told, at one of Elie Wiesel's lectures about biblical, talmudic, and Hasidic stories at the 92nd Street Y in New York City, I wept at the end. Then, years later, when I heard Wiesel tell this story while laughing and smiling, I laughed and smiled too. Rabbi Hanoch Teller, who tells true modern stories to convey inspirational truths, says that "the message of this story . . . has been instrumental in bringing countless couples to the bridal canopy." Such is the power of story! (Peninnah Schram)

The Hunchback

TRADITIONAL TALE RETOLD BY ZEV SHANKEN AND STEVE ZEITLIN[10]

A wealthy Berliner
hired Moses Mendelssohn, a founder of modern Judaism
and a hunchback,
to tutor his beautiful daughter.

Certainly, a man with such a deformity
would pose no temptation to his daughter.

But they fell in love all the same
because Mendelssohn told her
the following story:

Forty days before we were both conceived, there was a heavenly pronouncement:
"This man is to marry that woman."

And right then there came another announcement:
"But one of them is to be a hunchback."

And my soul said,
"Oh, my God, if one of us is to be a hunchback, let it be me."

COMMENTARY: In my travels as a folklorist, meeting husband-and-wife storytellers Abe Lass and Sylvia Cole was among my greatest pleasures. Abe was the last living piano player of the silent movies recorded for posterity by Folkways Records. Sylvia had written a beautiful memoir. To me, this tale says so much about the roles of women and men in shtetl life—and confronts them with humor. (Steve Zeitlin)

Another tale of shtetl life comes to mind. A man comes to the rabbi with a business proposition. Perplexed by the offer, the rabbi tells him, "Return the next day for my answer." Moments after he leaves, the rabbi goes over to his wife in the kitchen: "Malka, I need your advice." Explaining the dilemma, he asks, "How should I respond?" Malka looks at her husband and says, "What do I know, with my woman's brain?" Then, after a few moments, she continues, "But, Chaim, *if I were you*, here's what I would do." (Peninnah Schram)

A Cold Ass

ADAPTED BY STEVE ZEITLIN FROM AN INTERVIEW WITH
TEACHER AND MEMOIRIST SYLVIA COLE[11]

On a snowy night, two shtetl wives are returning home
from a hard day of work at the market,
when one of them, Norah, sees a candle burning in her second-story window,
and her husband, Yakob, swaying back and forth, studying Torah,
while she still has a table to set.
Suddenly she lifts her skirts,
squishes and rubs her behind around in the snow.
What are you doing, Norah? cries her friend.
That's so crass.
Norah replies, *Yakob is studying Torah*
while I'm working my tuchas *off at the market?*
And with a jerk of her head toward the window, she says,
Ikh zol im nokh aheymbrengen a varemenen tukhes oykn?
I should bring him home a warm ass yet?

COMMENTARY: One of the eminent Jewish matriarchs of modern times, Glückel of Hameln (1646–1724) wrote her memoirs primarily to help ease her sorrow after her husband's death. Yet she also addressed the memoirs to her children, so as to teach them, without seeming to preach, how to lead a moral Jewish life. As if "talking" to her children, she began by saying, "We should put ourselves to great pains for our children, for on this the world is built. Yet we must understand that if children did as much for their parents, the children would quickly tire of it."[13]

The Memoirs of Glückel of Hameln is an "ethical will." Not to be confused with a legal will, in which a person indicates how to allocate material things to family members, friends, and organizations, an ethical will transmits a spiritual legacy: one's wisdom and lessons for living. This Jewish tradition began with the biblical Jacob blessing his children and giving them his wisdom about how they should live after his death. In modern times, an ethical will is often composed in the form of memoirs or letters to one's children. Filled with personal reflections and experiences, it is a spiritual portrait of who you are. Ultimately, it is rooted in the premise that our deepest treasures are not to be found in the material objects we leave behind but rather in the teachings and blessings we bequeath to the next generation. (Peninnah Schram)

An Offspring's Answer

ADAPTED BY PENINNAH SCHRAM AND STEVE ZEITLIN
FROM *THE MEMOIRS OF GLÜCKEL OF HAMELN* [12]

One mother can take care of ten children,
but ten children can't take care of one mother.

After her husband died, Glückel responded to this old adage
with a fable for her children:

A mother bird knew that it was time
to migrate across a giant sea,
her fledgling on her back,
gingerly, watchfully.

My dear, sweet fledgling,
when I get old, tell me true:
Will you fly me across this massive sea,
as I do now for you?

I cannot promise, Mother dear,
to fly you across the sea,
because my own children may be riding on my back,
just as you are doing for me.

The Cart

ADAPTED BY STEVE ZEITLIN FROM A SUMMER CAMP
STORY TOLD BY RABBI DAVID HOLTZ[14]

While moving to Shpola,
Moishe sits beside his father on a horse-drawn cart
piled high with their possessions.
Suddenly, the cart skids on a rock,
lands in a ditch, sinks into the sand and sludge.

Tate, Father, says Moishe, *stand aside.*
I've got this in hand.

Moishe pushes the cart from behind.
It will not budge.

Son, you're missing something, says his Tate.

Moishe searches the underbrush,
finds a long branch.
Aha! I've got it, he says.
He puts the lever under the wheel,
gives it a nudge.
The cart sinks farther down in the sand.

There's something you haven't thought of,
his father reprimands.

Moishe finds a flat rock, jams it under a wheel,
pushes against the cart.
Still stuck.

What am I missing, Tate? he asks, exasperated.

You forgot to request a helping hand.

Blessing the New Moon in Wintertime

ADAPTED BY STEVE ZEITLIN FROM THE POEM BY
FOLK PAINTER RACHEL RAY LEHRER FAUST[15]

When the astronauts
made their first steps on the moon,
a scene from my Eastern European childhood came to mind.
Blessing the new moon on a winter's night,
a freezing, frosted night,
the roofs white with snow,
a circle of Jews stand,
prayer books in their hands,
eyes looking to the moon.

In that circle of Jews
I see my father.
The Jews are
the oldest astronauts.

COMMENTARY: Around the time of the first moonwalk, in 1969, Rachel Ray Lehrer Faust wrote a poem about the ancient Jewish ritual *Kiddush Levanah* (the monthly blessing of the new moon), as she experienced it as a child. Long before the moon became a place humans could visit, Jews were sanctifying it each month in its new phase. Its cycles were reminiscent of the historical phases of the Jewish people, who, as the Birnbaum siddur (daily prayer book) puts it, reappear after being eclipsed. And so, Faust is saying, the moon—a gift of the Creator, an object of ritual, the source of the calendar, and a reflection of the Jewish people—has been properly Jewish turf millennia before there were footprints on it.[16] (Steve Zeitlin)

COMMENTARY: There are variants of this folktale based on the tradition of the *maggid*, a storytelling rabbi who would travel from town to town to various shuls for a Shabbat or a *yom tov* (holiday) and deliver the *dvar Torah* (sermon focusing on the Torah portion). When this tale was told, the teller would usually swap out the storytelling rabbi for the well-known rabbi or *maggid* of that area—sometimes the famous Maggid of Dubno or the Baal Shem Tov. No matter who the rabbi was, the message was the same: the *balagola*, an ordinary Jew who drives the carriage, is also capable of resourceful, quick thinking to get out of a tight situation and outwit even the rabbi of the town. (Peninnah Schram)

The Rabbi and the *Balagola*

TRADITIONAL FOLKTALE RETOLD BY STEVE ZEITLIN[17]

A coachman—a *balagola*—carried the rabbi from shul to shul
through the shtetls of the Polish countryside.

Rabbi, he said, *I hear you give the same speech again and again.*
I've heard it so many times,
I could deliver it myself. No one would know.

The rabbi agreed to change places with his *balagola*—
To give you a chance, he said.

So the rabbi drove the coach from town to town,
and the *balagola* delivered the sermons.

One day, a local rabbi quizzed the "rabbi"
on a piece of talmudic minutiae,
a strange halakhic ruling from the commentaries,
a question above and beyond.

Aha, he said. *That is such a simple question—*
such a simple question!
So simple that even my balagola *here can respond.*

COMMENTARY: This story opens up various possible explanations and also questions. Was the townspeople's recollection of what had taken place at that seder only wishful thinking? Does Elijah the Prophet, the master of disguise, have to look like a person? Does "appearance" have to be external—why not internal? Finally, why do we have to open the door for Elijah the Prophet when he can do all kinds of miraculous things? To that, my father would explain, we have to get up, go forward, and open the door to welcome our guest. This way, we participate in helping miracles come true. We become partners with Elijah the Prophet. (Peninnah Schram)

Elijah

ADAPTED BY STEVE ZEITLIN FROM A TRADITIONAL
TALE TOLD BY FOLKLORIST AMY SHUMAN, BASED
ON A TELLING BY FOLKLORIST DOV NOY[18]

All through Eastern Europe each Passover eve,
shtetl doors opened in anticipation of Elijah . . .
but in all of history, it was said,
the great prophet had never graced a doorway.

Finally, one Passover in the shtetl of Shpola,
word circulated: *Tonight will be different from all other nights.*
At Reb Shmuel's house
the prophet will finally appear.

A bearded, burly writer bearing gifts
knocked upon the door.
I'm from the next village. May I join your seder
to witness the prophet's arrival?

Of course. Come in, dear traveler.

The seder proceeded through the lamb shank, the salt water, the bitter herbs,
the *haroset*, the four questions, the four cups of wine.

The door was opened for the seer.
The seder concluded, and the writer observed
Elijah's absence yet another year.

The next day the village was in a hubbub.
Did you hear? At Reb Shmuel's home last night,
the prophet Elijah appeared!

Parable of the Horse

ADAPTED BY STEVE ZEITLIN FROM A RETELLING
BY STORYTELLER JACK TEPPER[19]

Bedecked with jewels
and a gold-inlaid saddle,
the czar's horse, wandering through the forest alone,
encountered a large brown bear.

What are you? asked the bear.

I carried the czar in his inaugural procession.

Really, what are you? asked the bear.

I carried the fair czarina on her rides down forest paths.

But what are you?

What am I? I'm a horse.

And so, as a matter of course,
the bear devoured the horse.

Who Said the Jews Killed Jesus?

ADAPTED BY STEVE ZEITLIN FROM AN ORAL HISTORY
BY YIDDISH ACTOR BARUCH LUMET[20]

One Christmas where I grew up,
my town sparkled with beautiful white flowers
and windows covered with ice.
Children in long white gowns made of sheets,
with wings and paper crowns,
walked from house to house,
singing Christmas carols.
I was enchanted.

When the children went into a neighbor's house,
I followed them, asking,
Can I come in and listen to them sing?

No, our neighbor said. *You cannot come in.
You're Jewish. You killed our God.*

And that was the first time I heard that,
You killed our God.

It hurt me, deep inside,
so I asked my father,
What does she mean that we killed their God?

He said, *Don't listen to her. We didn't kill any God.
A God cannot be killed.*

The Hasid

TRADITIONAL JOKE

An exhausted Hasid
came running to his rebbe.
You must take pity on me. My house is afire.

The rebbe calmed the Hasid.
Then, fetching his stick from a corner of the room, he said,
Here, take this stick.
Run back to your home,
*draw circles around it, each one approximately seven handbreadths from
   the last one.*
At the seventh circle, step back seven handbreadths,
then lay this stick down at the west end of the fire.
God will surely help you.

The Hasid grabbed his stick and started off.
Listen, the rebbe called after him,
it wouldn't hurt also to throw water.
Water, water, as much water as you can!

A Nineteenth-Century Hasid Contemplates the Modern World

LINED OUT FROM A STORY ABOUT THE TEACHINGS OF
NINETEENTH-CENTURY REBBE ABRAHAM YAAKOV OF
SAGADORA, AS RECOUNTED BY MARTIN BUBER[21]

You can learn something from everything.
Everything can teach you something,
and not only everything God has created,
but also what man has made has something to teach us.

What can we learn from a train? one Hasid asked dubiously.

That because of one second, one can miss everything.

And from the telegraph?

That every word is counted and charged.

And from the telephone?

That what we say here is heard there.

COMMENTARY: I first heard this joke from Ruth Rubin, the Yiddish folk singer and ethnomusicologist. I loved the way she told it, and so I retold it often. Once, while searching for a specific story in Nathan Ausubel's anthology *A Treasury of Jewish Folklore*, I came across the same joke, called "Philosophy with Noodles"—a lovely title I borrowed for this version.[22]

It was a Jewish tradition for matchmakers to carry an umbrella as a symbol of their profession. This is dramatized in *Fiddler on the Roof*: the matchmaker carries an umbrella while endeavoring to arrange matches for Tevye's five daughters. Why matchmakers carried umbrellas is not clear, but I can speculate: When matchmakers finished making a good match, they might have opened and lifted the umbrella over the heads of the soon-to-be bride and groom—the umbrella taking the place of the future *huppah*—and then recited a blessing over the new couple. (Peninnah Schram)

Philosophy with Noodles

TRADITIONAL JOKE RETOLD BY PENINNAH SCHRAM

One day, a trusted matchmaker approached a shy young Hasid.

Chaim, she said, *I have the perfect match for you. I'll arrange a meeting.*

Chaim began to shake with fear. He turned to the matchmaker.

Please, Yentl, tell me: What should I say to her? What should I talk about?

The matchmaker, holding on to her umbrella, although the sun was
shining, laughed gently. *Chaim, there are three subjects to talk about, in
this order: food, family, philosophy.*

When the day came, the young Hasid was sitting at a table with the
young woman.

She, too, was nervous and looked down at the table, waiting.

Chaim tried to remember the wisdom of the matchmaker, the first subject.

Do you love noodles?

The young woman looked up and said simply, *No!*

Moments went by—not so quickly—and then Chaim remembered the
second subject.

Do you have a brother?

Once more, the young woman looked at Chaim and answered, *No!*

Ay! Ay! Ay! Now what was that third subject? Ah yes, philosophy.

Chaim straightened his shoulders with confidence and asked,

If you had a brother, would he have loved noodles?

COMMENTARY: After hearing me tell this tale at one of my synagogue programs, a gentleman, a psychiatrist, told me it had triggered the memory of the following true story.

After the psychiatrist had completed his studies, the doctors in a psychiatric hospital were giving him a tour when they stumbled upon a woman lying on the floor. He asked his hosts why she was lying on the floor. The hosts replied, "We don't know. And no one can get her to stand up."

"So I got down on the floor," he said, "and stretched out parallel to this woman—put my clenched hand under my cheek so my head was up—and asked her why she was there lying on the floor." Then, without waiting, I said to her: "I'll tell you what. I'll get up—and then you'll get up."

And I stood up—and, yes, the woman got up too.

In his comprehensive tome *A Palace of Pearls*, Howard Schwartz retells the story of the Rooster Prince and quotes Rabbi Nachman of Breslov: "In this way the genuine teacher must go down to the level of the students, if he wishes to raise them up."[24] (Peninnah Schram)

The Rooster Prince

ADAPTED BY STEVE ZEITLIN FROM A TRADITIONAL TALE
ATTRIBUTED TO RABBI NACHMAN OF BRESLOV[23]

A young prince decided he was a rooster.
He sat naked beneath the table,
flapped his arms like wings.

The king was despondent,
sent for the greatest doctors, to no avail.

One day an unknown Sage
approached the king
and received permission to speak to the son.

Undressing, he joined
the king's naked son beneath the table,
pretended to flap his wings, and said,
I am a rooster just like you.

Then the Sage put on a shirt.

Are you forgetting who you are?
The king's son winced.
Do you want to dress like a man?

You can put on a shirt and still be a rooster, said the Sage.
You can even wear a pair of pants and still be a rooster.

Then the Sage sent for food.
Again, the king's son winced.

You can eat what you want and still be a rooster, said the Sage.
You can act like a man and still be a rooster.

So the king's son resumed his former life,
for now it began to make sense:
you can be a rooster and still be a prince.

COMMENTARY: Elie Wiesel notes that "among the thousands of Hasidic leaders, great and small, from the Baal Shem's time to the Holocaust," Rebbe Menachem-Mendel of Kotzk "is undeniably the most disconcerting, mysterious figure of all. Also the most tragic. . . . He left no portrait, no personal possessions. . . . On his deathbed he was still obsessed that his writing might survive him." He questioned an old friend, "Have you searched everywhere? In all the hiding places? Are you sure everything is burned? That everything is ashes?"[26]

As this book certainly attests, I take a very different view. I've always loved the perspective of author Brenda Ueland: "I understood that writing was this: an impulse to share with other people a feeling or truth that I myself had. Not to preach to them, but to give it to them if they cared to hear it. If they did not—fine. . . . And I would never fall into those two extremes (both lies) of saying: 'I have nothing to say and am of no importance and have no gift'; or 'The public doesn't want good stuff.'"[27] (Steve Zeitlin)

Publishing

LINED OUT FROM A TRADITIONAL TALE BY THE EARLY
NINETEENTH-CENTURY REBBE MENACHEM-MENDEL
OF KOTZK, AS RETOLD BY ELIE WIESEL[25]

As Elie Wiesel tells the story, Rebbe Menachem-Mendel of Kotzk (1787–1859) tried to condense the entire human story into a single page he called "The Book of Man." He wrote the story down each day and tore it up each night.

So you know why I don't publish anything? he asked a visitor.
I'll tell you why.
Who would read me?
Not the scientists, not the scholars; they know more than I do.
To wish to read me, a man would have to feel that he knows less than I.
Who might that be?
A poor villager who works hard all week.
When would he have the time to open a book?
On Shabbat. When, at what time?
Not on Friday night; he would be too tired.
Saturday morning?
Reserved for services.
Then he comes home at midday, enjoys his meal, rushes
through the customary songs, and goes to lie down on his sofa,
at peace with himself.
Finally, he has a chance to glance at a book. He takes mine; he opens it.
But he has eaten too much; he feels heavy. He gets drowsier
by the minute; he falls asleep,
and here is my volume falling from his hands. And is it for him—for that—
that I should publish a book?

My answer is yes.

The Teller of Tales

TRADITIONAL TALE RETOLD BY RABBI EDWARD
SCHECTER AND MARC KAMINSKY[28]

There was once a Jew in Poland
who sought to make a living
telling tales. He spent six months studying
with the Baal Shem Tov, and left
overflowing with stories,
only to discover—there were few to listen.

One night at an inn, he heard
of a reclusive but generous Polish nobleman
who paid handsomely for tales.

In the castle,
at the end of a long table,
the nobleman sat stone-faced. The storyteller
told tale after tale.
When the nobleman heard one he'd never heard,
he pushed over a kopek, begrudgingly.

The storyteller got up to leave.
The nobleman asked, *Is that all?*

There is one more, just one more:

> *One day, when I was studying with the Baal Shem Tov,*
> *a man came to him, very upset.*
> *"Master of the Good Name," he said, "I was once a Jew,*
> *but the outside world, with its knowledge and possessions, beckoned.*
> *I felt constrained by Jewish tradition, and in order to partake of it all,*
>   *I converted.*
> *Now I am rich and successful, but forlorn. What shall I do?"*

"Do not worry, my son," said the Baal Shem Tov. *"Use your good fortune and knowledge*
    to help the orphan, the widow, and the stranger."

The nobleman nodded as he pushed over the kopek, gently now.
When will I know I have been forgiven?

As the Besht taught me on that fateful day, said the storyteller,

You will know you are forgiven
when you hear your story told.

COMMENTARY: The Baal Shem Tov, often called by the acronym "the Besht," founded the Hasidic movement by traveling from one town to another preaching his ideas: that all are equal, that purity of heart is superior to study, that joy rather than sadness should dominate one's relationship to God. He taught these ideas especially through stories and songs and spurred a revival of the Hasidic storytelling traditions. (Peninnah Schram)

This tale contains so much that is dear to the Jewish tradition: the importance of words, the telling of stories to set humankind free, the waiting, the wandering, the longing for redemption, the concept of a miracle for humans, by humans. Also, the belief that somewhere a human being waits and another human being pursues him. They don't even know each other, but when they meet, their lives will never be the same. (Rabbi Edward Schecter)

The Temples Rise

ADAPTED BY STEVE ZEITLIN FROM A TALE RETOLD
BY STORYTELLER ROSLYN BRESNICK-PERRY

The elders in the shtetl of Shpola stood on the dirt floor of their humble shul,
prayed for the coming of the Messiah.

Dig deep in your pockets,
said the rabbi to the wealthy elders in the front row.
Our shul should have a floor like all the others.

When the Messiah arrives, they cried, *we'll have a floor!*

Can you help?
said the rabbi to a traveling storyteller, the *maggid.*
You have a way with words. Our shul should have a floor.

The *maggid* stood at the head of the congregation and waved his hands.
He complimented the elders on their dedication to the Messiah.

My friends, he said, *on that fateful day,*
when Elijah blows the ram's horn, signals the coming of the Messiah
and the ingathering of the far-flung communities of exile to Jerusalem,
all the synagogues in the Pale of Settlement will rise up
and fly to their sacred places in the Holy City,

and, yes, this humble shul shall rise up too,
and you—the elders of the Temple—will remain right on this spot, standing
  on the dirt.

The next day, the wealthy elders dug deep into their pockets,
sprang for the floor.

COMMENTARY: In 1981 I was invited to host a cable television pilot series on storytelling. "Will there be guests?" I asked. "Yes," the producer said. "What will we talk about?" "Whatever you want to." "What is the show titled?" "*Conversations over a Glass Tea*." Immediately, I knew who my first guest would be: Lucjan Dobroszycki, the Polish historian who survived the Łódź ghetto and was always a delightful conversationalist. While sitting around the table, each of us with a glass of tea, Lucjan suddenly recalled this story. (Peninnah Schram)

Conversations over a Glass of Tea

TRADITIONAL TALE RETOLD BY PENINNAH SCHRAM

On the lace-draped tables of the wealthy,
a magnificent samovar held a place of honor,
fine glasses of tea nestled in silver holders,
and, at center stage, a cut-glass bowl was filled with sugar cubes.

When people at the table wished to take a sip of tea,
they would take a sugar cube,
break it between their teeth,
hold it in their mouths,
sip the tea through the sugar.

The Polish people had a word for that: *złamać*, "to break."

On the linen-lined tables of the comfortable-but-not-wealthy,
a nice samovar was present,
glasses of tea sat in metal holders,
and, at center stage, a nice glass plate was filled with sugar cubes.

When people at that table wished to take a sip of tea,
they would look at the sugar cubes
and drink the tea.

The Polish people had a word for that: *patrzeć*, "to look."

On the cotton-clothed tables of the poor
stood a plain metal samovar,
tea in plain naked glasses,
and, at center stage, a simple dish—empty.

When people at the table wished to take a sip of tea,
they would look at the dish
and imagine the sugar cubes.

The Polish people had a word for that: *wyobrazić*, "to imagine."

COMMENTARY: Years ago, when I first heard someone read this classic story in Yiddish, it was so poignant that I burst out weeping. At the end, when Bonshe Schweig is in heaven and is asked to request whatever he wants, he keeps on repeating one word, *Takeh!* (Really!), in various tones of disbelief. So much is in that one word! The judge finally convinces Bonshe that he can indeed choose anything he wants and it will be given to him. He could have asked for world peace or a just society or enough food for everyone and on and on . . . Yet how could he? He had lived such an unhappy, unacknowledged life. It's as if he'd worn blinders, like the horses. Perhaps there's a bit of Bonshe Schweig in each of us. (Peninnah Schram)

Fresh Rolls and Butter

BY ZEV SHANKEN, INSPIRED BY THE SHORT STORY
"BONTSHE SHVAYG" BY I. L. PERETZ[29]

In the Peretz telling of the tale, Bonshe Schweig was always picked on—
even his name means "be quiet" in Yiddish.
When he gets to heaven, he is offered his reward:
one wish—any wish—that the angels promise will come true.

He thinks and thinks and clarifies. *Anything at all?*
Really? Anything?
Finally, he says, *Each morning, if it's not too much trouble,*
I would like—and then he thinks some more.
Finally, he says,
I would like fresh, warm rolls with butter.

Fresh rolls with butter?
The angels are stunned
at this ghetto Jew's imagination,
eviscerated by centuries of oppression.

There is much to denigrate about the old ghetto Jew.
They hated much of it themselves.
But when I look back on this tale from a different place—
postmodern, post-Zionist, post-assimilationist—
I ask myself,
Did perhaps Bonshe Schweig understand
there's something heavenly about fresh, warm rolls with butter
each morning till the end of time?

COMMENTARY: Born in 1916, Mayer Kirshenblatt left Opatów, Poland, in 1934. Six decades later, the seventy-three-year-old former housepainter, then living in Toronto, began to paint his memories on canvas. In the book *They Called Me Mayer July: Painted Memories of a Jewish Childhood in Poland before the Holocaust*, cowritten with his folklorist daughter Barbara Kirshenblatt-Gimblett, Mayer shares paintings and stories about the characters in his hometown. He was a child witness to the kinds of people who populated shtetls in much of Eastern Europe. Mayer died in 2009. (Steve Zeitlin)

How We Lived: A Tribute to Mayer Kirshenblatt

ADAPTED BY STEVE ZEITLIN AND MARC KAMINSKY FROM *THEY CALLED ME MAYER JULY* BY STORYTELLER AND PAINTER MAYER KIRSHENBLATT AND BARBARA KIRSHENBLATT-GIMBLETT[30]

Hey! There was a big world out there before the Holocaust
in my hometown of Opatów,
where the fastest thing we knew was the speed of a horse.

When he slowed down, his daughter Barbara and her husband, Max
convinced the seventy-three-year-old former housepainter living in Toronto
to paint his memories on canvas—
child witness to a remembered world.

The first was of his mother's kitchen, where the soup pot never left the stove;
then the acrobat, the organ grinder, and the cellist in Mandelbaum's courtyard;
the cobbler's son, whose family dressed him in white pajamas resembling a
    burial shroud
to foil the angel of death into thinking he was already dead;
Ludwig, the water carrier, bringing buckets from the town well,
where the water wasn't as good as the water from the well of Harshl—
known as the Stuffed Intestine;
the cholera epidemic that came to an end when the town held a wedding in
    the cemetery,
encouraging the recently departed to intervene with the Holy One;
the prostitute showing off her wares near Zajfman's Tavern;
the boys exchanging the butcher shop's with the barbershop's sign,
and watching through the window the Purim play performed for a wealthy family,
peering longingly at the food on the tables and the nibbles on the side;
the kleptomaniac with a fish down her bosom that she'd cribbed,
all of them conferred to canvas in vivid color, with exactitude to assuage
    the worry
that future generations might remember more about how Jews died
than how they lived.

4 JEWels . . . *in Jokes*

Beyond the meager possessions bundled in their arms as they sailed into New York Harbor at the turn of the century, Jewish immigrants brought their indomitable sense of humor and storytelling, the culture of *Yiddishkeit*. As that culture intermingled with the prevailing U.S. folk culture, Jewish humor became synonymous with New York humor—and, through early television, with American humor. Via comedians such as Jack Benny, Milton Berle, Fanny Brice, Lenny Bruce, George Burns, Mort Sahl, Sam Levenson, Buddy Hackett, Jackie Mason, Myron Cohen, Don Rickles, Joan Rivers, the Marx Brothers, Henny Youngman, Woody Allen, and Jon Stewart, Jews have left an indelible imprint on American humor.[1] "There is a Jewish joke for every problem," the poet Annie Lanzillotto once told me.

Jews have long understood that laughter often opens and focuses the mind on more serious teachings. As the Talmud (Shabbat 30b) states, before beginning a lesson, the teacher should introduce humor—a story or a joke.

But just as the youngest child at the seder asks, "Why is this night different from all other nights?" Jewish scholars, writers, comedians, and thinkers have long asked, "Why is Jewish humor different from all other kinds of humor?"[2]

My own attempt at the answer always begins with talmudic reasoning— Jewish jokes rooted in a peculiar kind of convoluted logic. Many Jewish writers and storytellers point to their favorite examples. Social scientist and humorist

Leo Rosten tells of a letter he received from comedian Groucho Marx. It began, "Dear Junior: Please excuse me for not answering your letter sooner. But I have been so busy not answering letters lately that I have not been able to get around to not answering yours in time."[3]

Another characteristic feature of a Jewish joke is questioning. Why must a Jew always answer a question with a question? Why not? After all, many of the greatest Jewish quotations are framed as philosophical questions, from Rabbi Hillel's "If I am only for myself, who will be for me? If I am only for myself, what am I? If not now, when?"[4] to Sholem Aleichem's "God, I know we are your chosen people, but couldn't you choose somebody else for a change?"[5]

Moshe gets a crash course in questioning after he reads this sign outside a Lower East Side tailor shop:

> *My name is Fink*
> *So what do you think—*
> *I press clothes for nothing.*

He gets his shirts together, brings them in, comes back a few days later, and much to his surprise, along with his shirts there's a hefty bill.

"What about the sign?" Moshe accuses the tailor. "It says you press clothes for nothing."

"Oh no," the tailor says, pulling Moshe outside to look at the sign. "You're reading it all wrong. It says,

> *My name is Fink,*
> *So what do you think?*
> *I press clothes for nothing?"*

The playwright Bertolt Brecht once wrote, "He who laughs has not yet heard the bad news." The folks who told the jokes that follow—and the author of this book, who had the chutzpah to recast them all as poems—laugh as if they haven't yet heard the bad news: antisemitism, death, genocide, even circumcisions gone awry.

A great many Jews would join them in laughter. After all, when a 2013 Pew survey asked American Jews, "What's essential to being Jewish?," almost half of them answered, "Having a good sense of humor."[6] Jewish jokes themselves are proof of this concept. "What do you love most about me," Becky asks her husband, Abe, "my natural beauty or my gorgeous body?" Abe: "Your sense of humor."[7]

In the poems that follow, I invite you to come up with your own answer to the insoluble question "What—if anything—is distinctive about Jewish humor?"

Passementerie

TRADITIONAL TALE ADAPTED BY STEVE ZEITLIN
FROM A TELLING BY JACK TEPPER[8]

Sam Cohen is a salesman of ribbons and notions—passementerie—very
   successful,
and after forty years, he is going to retire.
Talking to another salesman, he says,
You know Mr. O'Connell, who owns a dress house?
He would never buy anything from me because he hates Jews.
The highlight of my career would be if, before I retire, I could sell him an
   order.

So he goes to Mr. O'Connell.

Mr. O'Connell looks at him and says sardonically,
I hear you're retiring, Cohen. You've been bothering me for years,
and you know I don't deal with Hebes.
But, okay, you want an order, I'll give you an order—you got any red ribbon?

Cohen says, *Sure, we got red ribbon. What width?*

He says, *Half-inch.*

We got half-inch ribbon. How much you need?

Well, I want a ribbon that will reach from your belly button to the tip of
   your penis.
That's as big a piece of ribbon as I want.
And Mr. O'Connell throws him out of his factory.

Six weeks later, Mr. O'Connell goes to his factory,
and in front of the door are five trailer trucks,
and they are unloading thousands and thousands of yards of ribbon.
He runs inside, gets on the phone, and says,
Cohen, you miserable animal: What did you send me?

Cohen says, *Look, Mr. O'Connell. Exactly what you asked for is what I*
   sent you.
My belly button—everybody knows where it is.
You said till it reaches the tip of my penis.
Sixty-five years ago I was circumcised,
in a little town outside of Warsaw, Poland . . .

COMMENTARY: To quote the punch line of an old joke, "Some people can tell them and some people can't." I've heard versions of this circumcision joke dozens of times. Jack Tepper is a master joke teller, a true raconteur. I sense the poetry in the rhythms and intonations of his speech. As the philosopher Steven Gimbel writes, jokes must be seen as individual works of art, created by particular human artists, even if—as with the cave paintings in Lascaux, France—the name of the artists are lost to history. (Steve Zeitlin)[9]

COMMENTARY: When I first heard this joke, it was a Russian in the first verse, a German in the second, and a Frenchman in the third. *Always* it's the Jew in that final verse.

Laughter is physically, mentally, and emotionally healing. Psychiatrist Donald W. Black wrote in the *Journal of the American Medical Association* that when one laughs with a belly laugh, it causes a physical change in the *kishkes* (a funny Yiddish word for "intestines" that when uttered often brings laughter in and of itself)—and that as a result of that belly laugh, one feels better.[11] Accompanying the article was an editorial by an expert in the field, in this case satirist Art Buchwald, who pointed to the "many unanswered questions" left by Dr. Black, "such as whether a person can laugh himself to death and why Medicare or Medicaid will not pay for laughter if it is such a good medicine."[12] (Peninnah Schram)

Telling Jokes in the Shtetl

TRADITIONAL JOKE[10]

When you tell a joke to a Russian peasant,
he laughs three times: once when you tell it to him,
the second time when you explain it,
and the third time when he understands it.

A landowner laughs only twice:
when he hears the joke and when you explain it,
for he can never understand it.

An army officer laughs only once:
when you tell the joke.
He never lets you explain it,
and that he is unable to understand it
goes without saying.

But the Jew—
before you've even had a chance to finish, he interrupts you impatiently.
First of all, he's heard it before.
Second, what business do you have telling a joke when you don't know how?
In the end, he decides to tell you the jest himself,
but in a much better version than yours.

My Mother Liked Telling Jokes

BY ESTHER COHEN

Born in Grand Forks,
North Dakota, Romanian parents
they snuck across
from Winnipeg, all of them told jokes.

My mother's favorite, she told it a thousand times:
An old Jewish woman just like her
was wearing her best bathing suit when she
strutted across the Florida sand. Probably
Miami, though it could have been
Boca Raton. Three men were sitting
on a bench facing the water, and she
walked right up to them. *If you
guess what's in my hand, you can have
sex with me*, she said. The man on the end
was first. *An elephant*, he said.
Close enough, she said.

Taxi

TRADITIONAL JOKE

Moishe is crossing Fifth Avenue when
a cab runs a red light
and knocks him down.

As a crowd gathers around him,
a gentleman takes off his own coat,
places it across Moishe's shoulders.

Are you comfortable? he asks.

I make a living, he says.

COMMENTARY: Some deeper ideas are embedded in this joke.
Many immigrant Jews, as well as many souls of every race and
creed, struggle to get by. Is Moishe suggesting that he makes a
living but not necessarily that he lives comfortably? Or is he say-
ing that he lives perfectly comfortably *because* he makes a living?
What does it mean to enjoy a comfortable life? We all need to
make a living—and a life. (Steve Zeitlin)

Einstein's Theory of Relativity

TRADITIONAL JOKE

Little Sammy told his grandfather,
Our teacher says that only a few people
in the whole world can really understand
Einstein's theory of relativity.
But then our teacher told us what it means.

Einstein's theory is like this:
if you have four hairs on your head, that's a little,
but if you have four hairs in your soup, that's a lot.

Grandpa slowly shakes his head.
Sammy, he says softly, *from this your Einstein makes a living?*

COMMENTARY: Jews have *shepped naches* (derived pride and joy) from Albert Einstein, a German Jew who became one of the greatest physicists of all time (and helped found the Hebrew University in Jerusalem). As such, he has become part of Jewish folklore. In this joke, Einstein's formative theory of relativity is reduced to a morsel of talmudic reasoning, akin to "If you sit on a hot stove for a minute it seems like an hour, but if you sit with a pretty girl for an hour it seems like a minute."

This story seems to prove an oft-cited quality of Jewish humor—that the punch line can work without the joke. When I finished one of my talks on Jewish humor one evening, an old man stood, shrugged, and asked the audience: "From this he makes a living?" (Steve Zeitlin)

Schwartz

TRADITIONAL JOKE

In Jewish tradition, the *hevra kadisha* committee
washes the bodies of the dead.

But Ned didn't expect
the corpse of Mr. Schwartz
to have a schlong
so long.

So he decided to tell his wife, Sadie—
then, what the hell,
sliced it off like a loaf of bread,
placed it in his briefcase to carry home instead.

Sadie, you won't believe what I saw at work today.

What did you see, Ned?

Just open the briefcase—and she did.

Oh my God, Schwartz is dead!

COMMENTARY: This is what's called a "narrative joke": a little
story that ends in a punch line. There's also what's called a "hid-
den narrative" within it—here, that Sadie is well acquainted with
this *member* of the congregation. (Bob Mankoff)

Abe and Becky

TRADITIONAL JOKE ADAPTED BY STEVE ZEITLIN FROM A
RETELLING BY EDUCATOR AND JOKE COLLECTOR HERB SHORE

When Abe and Becky quarreled,
she referred to him as Mr. Schwartz
and he to her by her maiden name, Mrs. Cohen.

Can you please turn out the light, Mr. Schwartz?
If you ask nicely, Mrs. Cohen.

Can you let me have some of the covers, Mr. Schwartz?
If you say thank you, Mrs. Cohen.

Would you please stop poking me with your elbow, Mr. Schwartz?

That's not my elbow.

Call me Becky.

COMMENTARY: Off-color jokes about the couple Abe and Becky
are often told and retold by Jewish seniors. At one talk I gave at a
Jewish senior center, Herb Shore told this joke and later handed
me four booklets of "Abe and Becky" jokes that he'd compiled.
This joke was my favorite, and a second favorite follows. (Steve
Zeitlin)

The Theater

TRADITIONAL JOKE ADAPTED BY STEVE ZEITLIN
FROM A RETELLING BY HERB SHORE

Why is it you don't enjoy the theater?
Becky asked Abe.

It's like this, he answers.

In act one, she wants him,
but he doesn't want her.

In act two, he wants her,
but she doesn't want him.

In act three, they finally want each other,
and the curtain comes down.

The Perfect Girl

TRADITIONAL JOKE[13]

A friend asks Abie,
How come you never married?

Simple, I never found the perfect girl.

*You mean you never found one girl
in this whole wide world
good enough for you?*

Only once, I did. I found the perfect girl.

Then why didn't you marry her?

She was looking for the perfect guy.

Two Old Jews at a Urinal

TRADITIONAL JOKE

A few years ago, I gave a talk on Jewish humor
at the Eldridge Street Synagogue in Lower Manhattan.
When it was over, I found myself in the bathroom,
standing beside a man who said he liked my jokes,
and that our situation reminded him of

two old Jews standing side by side at a urinal:
The first Jew's pee skews to the left,
splashes into the second man's urinal.

The second man's pee also sprays askew,
landing in the third urinal from the left.

Says one man to the other,
I guess Rabbi Schlemkee did your circumcision too.

COMMENTARY: My father was a *hazzan* (a cantor who chants
the liturgy), a *shoḥet* (a ritual slaughterer), and a *mohel* (one who
performs circumcision, removing the foreskin from a baby boy's
penis). In the "old country," men would be trained for these three
fields of work as their combined profession—yes, three profes-
sions practiced by one person.

In his role as *mohel*, my father would perform the bris
(Yiddish) or *brit milah* (Ashkenazi Hebrew) ceremony—both
words mean "covenant"—welcoming the baby boy into the cov-
enant with God as a member of the Jewish people and formally
giving him his Hebrew name (which was not shared until the
circumcision, on his eighth day of life). Unlike in the joke, I know
of no situations where the circumcision went awry. Always my
father drove to the site of the rite in his Packard—the Clipper
model. (Peninnah Schram)

Time Stamp

TRADITIONAL JOKE

Because Dropkin was the first in his class,
he had to deliver the speech to the grads.
At the podium, true to his nervous ways,
he dropped his papers, bumped his head on the mic,
bent over to reclaim what he had to deliver,
then cut a fart so loud his pants quivered.

Humiliated and spurned,
he left town
and never returned

till fifty years later, when his mother lay dying.
Under cover of night, he opened the hotel door
to find an eager young clerk inquiring,
Have you ever been to this town before?

Yes, he said, *I was born here,
but something happened to me that brought me low,
so I left this town
many years ago.*

Ah, said the clerk. *You felt you had to depart.
But it probably wasn't that bad.
The town is very forgiving—at its heart.*

Ah, said Dropkin, *that's good to know.
So who cares, anyway—it was a long, long time ago.*

How many years? the clerk asked.

About fifty. Ample time to restart.

*Was that before or after
the Dropkin fart?*

The Plotkin Diamond

TRADITIONAL JOKE

Mrs. Cohen sees her friend at the mall
with a gorgeous diamond on her ring finger.

Oh my, she says,
that is the most beautiful diamond I have ever seen.

It is a beautiful diamond, her friend says.
In fact, it's the world-famous Plotkin Diamond.

Really?

But it comes with a curse.

A curse? says Mrs. Cohen. *What curse?*

Plotkin.

Rich Man

TRADITIONAL JOKE

If I were a rich man,
I'd be as rich as Rockefeller, says Jacob.

Rich as Rockefeller? says Harry.

Rich as Rockefeller.

Well, says Harry, *if I were rich, I'd . . .*
be richer than Rockefeller.

Richer than Rockefeller? says Jacob.
How is that?

I'd do a little teaching on the side.

COMMENTARY: In the version Nathan Ausubel relates in *A Treasury of Jewish Folklore*, this joke is set in Chelm, the town of fools, and the speakers are two teachers.[14] After the Rothschilds built a European banking dynasty and became the wealthiest Jewish family worldwide, their name became symbolic of wealth, especially for Jews. In America, the name Rothschild was replaced by the name of a non-Jewish family, Rockefeller.

Perhaps Jews are not alone in needing billionaires to dream about, measure themselves against, and make fun of. In this case, Harry imagines himself a billionaire who still chooses to hold down a low-paying job as a teacher. Then again, there are probably a number of Jews who would do just that. (Peninnah Schram)

Golda

TRADITIONAL JOKE RETOLD AS A CLEVER COMEBACK BY GOLDA MEIR

At a meeting in Jerusalem, Golda Meir,
prime minister of Israel,
asks Henry Kissinger, U.S. secretary of state,
when the F10 fighter jets Israel needs will be delivered.

Hold on, Golda, Kissinger says.
You have to understand:
I am, first and foremost, a citizen of the United States.
Second, I am a citizen of the world.
And third, I am a Jew.

Ah, yes, Henry, Golda says.
But, you see, in Israel
we read from right to left.

COMMENTARY: Golda Meir, who served as Israel's prime minister from 1969 to 1974, was renowned for her quotable phrases on Jewish history. "Let me tell you something that we Israelis have against Moses. He took us 40 years through the desert in order to bring us to the one spot in the Middle East that has no oil."[15] And "As for Jews being a chosen people, I never quite accepted that. It seemed, and still seems to me, more reasonable to believe not that God chose the Jews, but that the Jews were the first people that chose God, the first people in history to have done something truly revolutionary, and it was that choice that made them unique."[16] I appreciate this sentiment, as it suggests a less problematic reason Jews may choose to think about themselves as the "chosen people." (Steve Zeitlin)

The Commandments

TRADITIONAL JOKE ADAPTED BY STEVE ZEITLIN FROM A
TELLING BY CATSKILLS COMIC RUBIN LEVINE[17]

Moses
went up to the mountain.

God says,
I have some commandments for you.

Moses says,
How much are they?

God says,
They're free.

So Moses says,
I'll take ten.

COMMENTARY: I met Rubin Levine when he was playing the
violin and cracking one-liners at Sammy's Roumanian Steakhouse
on New York's Lower East Side. I also saw him playing for tips
while I stood in line for a Broadway show. Although he never
became famous, he worked for many years in the Jewish Catskills
resorts and embodied Borscht Belt humor. "A Jew," he once told
me, "goes into Katz's Deli and orders a ham sandwich. The man
behind the counter says, 'I can't do that, because every time I
serve a ham sandwich, somewhere in the world a Jew dies.'"
(Steve Zeitlin)

Perfect

TRADITIONAL JOKE RETOLD BY PENINNAH SCHRAM

Shirley and Irv have a baby boy, but they're worried—
he never speaks.
In six months, one year, two years—he never speaks.

From all the doctors and specialists, it's the same story:
There is nothing to prevent this child's speech.
But in five years, ten years, twenty years—he never speaks.

Then, one day, when their boy is twenty-one,
at the dinner table, dipping a spoon into the soup,
he throws the spoon. *This soup stinks!*

Overjoyed, Shirley and Irv run over.
My son, my son, you can speak!
Why didn't you speak all these years?

Up till now, he says,
everything was perfect!

Toyota

TRADITIONAL JOKE

Sadie's husband died.
She'd never cared about him anyway.

Her friends told her,
You really should put something in the paper for Herbie.

So she calls the *Forward*, the Jewish paper.
This is Sadie. How much for an obit?

The lady from the newspaper says,
Ten dollars for five words.

Okay, says Sadie. Put this in:
"Herbie died."

But, Sadie, you get five words for ten dollars.
You get three more words.

Okay, put this in:
"Herbie died. Toyota for sale."

COMMENTARY: I remember sitting with my father and brothers over dinner the night my mother, Shirley, passed away, in 1999. We sat in stunned, awkward silence, when somehow the line "Toyota for sale" popped into my mind, and I said it aloud. The three of us laughed so hard we cried. The darker the situation, the blacker the humor needs to be. (Steve Zeitlin)

Worry

TRADITIONAL TALE

In Chelm, the town of fools,
Shmuel was known as a poor man, a worrier,
and the town had more than its share of worries.

One day the wise elders of Chelm
devised a new idea:
Why don't we pay Shmuel a ruble a year
to worry for us all?

Shmuel was excited by the prospect.
The elders rushed to pass the law
to eradicate all worry—

but then the wisest of the fools protested:
We've got to think this out.
If we pay Shmuel a ruble a year to worry,
what would he have to worry about?

COMMENTARY: The philosophical *summum bonum* and the deeply earthly pleasures of sex are brought together in this tale. Much Jewish humor emerges from two opposing qualities of the Jewish psyche—a philosophical bent and a practical mind— which constantly undercut each other. It's as if Jews have their heads in the clouds and their feet mired in the tar of the Lower East Side. As one critic writing about the Jewish theater put it, "It reaches toward heaven but has dust on its shoes."[19]

Abe Lass once told me that Jews were so aware and proud of their culture that one could easily find in the holdings of Jewish archives any kind of cantorial singing as well as books on any aspect of Jewish history, including the general history of Jewish humor. The one element missing from these archives, he believed, was the dirty Yiddish joke. And so Abe took it upon himself to record seven hours of dirty Yiddish jokes for the City Lore archives.[20] (Steve Zeitlin)

The Summmum Bonum

TRADITIONAL JOKE ADAPTED BY STEVE ZEITLIN FROM
A PERSONAL RETELLING BY ABE LASS[18]

Each morning in the Garden cafeteria,
where it is said that seltzer squirted from the ornate fountain,
the over-eighty crowd gathered for breakfast,
and Harry, Irving, and Moishe inevitably discussed
the *summum bonum*, the "greatest good."

For me, Harry the butcher said, *the* summum bonum *is davening on
    Yom Kippur at the synagogue.*
That's when I truly feel cleansed of my sins.

For me, Irving the tailor said, *the* summum bonum *is coming home on a
    Friday evening*
and seeing the set Sabbath table, the challah, my wife lighting the candles.
I know the workweek is over and all is at peace.

For me, Moishe the salesman said, *the* summum bonum *was a trip I took
with my secretary to see a furniture showroom in Las Vegas.*
*When we got to the hotel we had sex, before we went to sleep we had sex,
and then in the morning we had sex again.*

Hold it, hold it, hold it right there, protested Harry and Irving.
That's not fair. We're talking "good"—you're talking "very good."

Zoom

BY WRITER AND HUMORIST MARC WALLACE

Put seventy-five Jews in a room,
trying to deal mit da Zoom.
One presses ah button,
she's left wit . . . nuttin'
and dis party's a busted balloon.

COMMENTARY: Being on Zoom for sometimes four to six hours a day during the COVID-19 pandemic, I coined a new Yiddish word: *oysgezoomt*, meaning "zoomed out." (Peninnah Schram)

Self-Critique

BY POET AND PROSE PROVOCATEUR SPARROW[21]

My
poems
are
failures
disguised
as jokes.

COMMENTARY: The intriguing short poems of Jewish iconoclast Sparrow have, for me, a decidedly talmudic quality. "What do they call the Jewish neighborhood of El Paso?" he writes. "El Passover." Once, at New York City's Nuyorican Poets Cafe he and I competed in a poetry slam against some of the cafe's most powerful slam poets. He read his short poem "Harmonica," which went simply: "Don't harm Monica." (Steve Zeitlin)

Jewish Mother Telegram

TRADITIONAL JOKE RETOLD BY ZEV SHANKEN

Start worrying. Details to follow.

A Freudian Analysis

ATTRIBUTED TO, AMONG OTHERS, *SATURDAY NIGHT LIVE* COMEDIAN
JULIA SWEENEY, WHO WROTE A BOOK WITH THIS TITLE[22]

If it's not one thing, it's your mother.

Jewish Mothers

TRADITIONAL JOKE

How many Jewish mothers
does it take to change a lightbulb?

None.
I'll just sit in the dark.

Twenty Years

TRADITIONAL JOKE[23]

A beloved scholar of the Talmud lay upon his deathbed.
The doctors did everything in their power to extend the man's life.
The rabbi of the town recited every healing prayer he knew.

Finally, the rabbi called the members of the congregation together.

I want each one of you to donate before God
a portion of the life allotted to you.

Men and women rose, one after the other.
Some donated a day, a week, a month.

Finally, Abe shouted out, *I donate twenty years—*

Are you crazy? cried the rabbi—

of my mother-in-law's life.

Seven Differences between a Joke and a Poem

BY ZEV SHANKEN

1. A joke is something your mother couldn't tell.
A poem is the same thing, but with your father.

2. Jokes don't get better the more you hear them.

3. The answer to a joke: "To get to the other side."
The answer to a poem: "To see time fly."

4. Freud never had to write a book called
Poems and Their Relation to the Unconscious.

5. A poem repeated is a grape fermented.

A joke repeated is a rotten banana.

6. You can kill a joke, but you can only knock a poem unconscious.

7. A joke never waits for you.

COMMENTARY: Everything about a joke has to be clear. Often there's ambiguity along the way—misdirection in the beginning— but at the end the ambiguity is always resolved. And it's always understood when you get it. You don't want that in a poem. If the words make you care, then it's a poem. If they make you laugh, you don't care as much—you have enough distance from the subject to laugh at it. Then it's a joke. (Bob Mankoff)

Optimism/Pessimism

TRADITIONAL JOKE

The Jewish pessimist:
Things can't get any worse.
The Jewish optimist:
Yes, they can get worse—much worse.
The optimist:
This is the best of all possible worlds.
The pessimist:
Unfortunately.
The optimist just before the end of the world:
At least it's not the end of the world.

COMMENTARY: It seems fitting that Jewish humorists should riff on optimism versus pessimism. The history of the Jews being subjected to exile and genocide has provided ample reason for them to totter on the verge of hopelessness and despair but to use as antidotes humor and hope. In his chapter "Jewish Humor: The Currency of Hope," David Arnow notes that humor helps us forge connections to the universe and see beyond what's staring us in the face.[24]

I consider myself an optimist. Someone once asked me why, then, am I not smiling all the time. "With all that's happening in the world," I said, "do you think it's easy to be an optimist?" (Steve Zeitlin)

5 JEWels . . . *from Torah*

"EACH PERSON HAS A TORAH, UNIQUE TO THAT PERSON, HIS OR HER innermost teaching," writes Rabbi Lawrence Kushner. "Some seem to know their Torahs very early in life and speak and sing them in a myriad of ways. Others spend their whole lives stammering, shaping, and rehearsing them. Some are long, some short. Some are intricate and poetic, others are only a few words, and still others can only be spoken through gesture and example. But every soul has a Torah. . . . For each soul, by the time of his or her final hour, the Torah is complete, the teaching done."[1]

In synagogues around the world, scrolls inscribed with the Five Books of Moses stand shoulder to shoulder in the *Aron Kodesh*, the ark positioned on the wall that faces Jerusalem. Because the weekly readings of scriptures are meticulously prescribed, almost every sermon delivered from the pulpit (and every talk given by a bar or bat mitzvah) draws on the given week's Torah portion as a parable of contemporary life. There is a sense in which each generation "parable-izes" the experiences revealed in the Torah.

Yet the Jewish tradition of learning that is Torah in a broader sense does not begin and end with the Five Books of Moses (Torah), the Talmud, and/or the commentaries that followed. Consider, as just one example among many, Jewish mythology. As Howard Schwartz notes in *Tree of Souls: The Mythology of Judaism*, Jewish mythology was reborn with the Kabbalah's offering of its own creation story (thirteenth century), extended by the kabbalist Rabbi Isaac Ben Solomon Luria (sixteenth century), and reborn again with the Baal Shem Tov and the Hasidic movement (nineteenth century).[2]

The Jewish experience of learning is also alive and well in those Jews who don't attend synagogue or connect to Kabbalah. Some of us, for instance, derive meaning from Jewish stories, jokes, and parables. The Jewish tradition of learning Torah is part of us all.

These poems from Torah, Adam and Eve, Abraham, Moses, and others help us think through problems, laugh, poke fun at human frailty, and imagine better worlds.

The *Tsimtsum*

BY RABBI EDWARD SCHECTER

Do you know the *tsimtsum*
that filled the fertile
void?

God has filled all space, God
is everywhere. God wants to create
the world, but there's no place
for the sublunar world. So God folds
into a *tsimtsum* of Herself, contracts
like a woman's womb, creates

an intensification of God—releases an explosive birth
of the stars, the earth. The universe
springs forth from the dark,
leaving a spark
of divinity in everything.

COMMENTARY: *Tsimtsum* (literally, "reduction") is a way of
being present in absence. According to Kabbalah, a *tsimtsum* is a
reduction of the divine energy that creates worlds.[3] The kabbal-
ists introduced this idea to explain how, since God's presence (or
infinite light) encompassed the entire universe, there could still
be room for creation[4]

My friend and possibly distant cousin Ariel Zeitlin, who has
explored the Zohar for a novel she is writing, emailed me to say,
"Once God birthed the cosmos, He created ten vessels to store
the holy sparks. Is it any wonder that He poured too much of His
essence into the vessel that held our own world as He was creat-
ing it? That vessel cracked in the process and so the world was
flawed in the very act of creation. Our job as humans is to live in
our broken world in such a way that we heal it."[5] (Steve Zeitlin)

Rabbi Simon Said

ADAPTED BY STEVE ZEITLIN FROM A MIDRASH IN
THE NAME OF RABBI SIMON JACOBSON[6]

As God was about to create the first humans,
the ministering angels argued.

Some of them said: *Let them be created.*

Some of them said: *Let them not be created.*

Lovingkindness said: *Let them be created, because they will perform acts
of lovingkindness.*

Truth said: *Let them not be created, for all will be falsehood.*

Justice said: *Let them be created, because they will do deeds of justice.*

Peace said: *Let them not be created, because life entails conflict.*

While the ministering angels were arguing,
God made the humans and said:
Why are you debating? The deed is done.

Hillel and Shammai

TRADITIONAL TALE RETOLD BY RABBI EDWARD SCHECTER

One evening, at the close of the Sabbath,
Rabbi Hillel and Rabbi Shammai took a long walk
to ponder the question of whether God might have considered resting
    on the sixth day,
sidestepped humanity, and avoided so much of the bloodshed, illness,
    and planetary devastation caused by human misdeeds.

The school of Shammai and the school of Hillel took up the debate.
Some argued that a world without humans would have improved the
    planet's fate.
Others said it was better for man to procreate and sow his seeds.

For two and a half years they argued,
until they declared:
Yes, *it would have been better if humankind had never been created,*
but, *given that we were created,*
all of us need be conscious of our deeds.

What I Would Tell Adam and Eve

BY POET FRANCINE WITTE

First of all, I'd show up naked and empty
of knowledge. The two things were never
connected. I'd rake the garden, clear
out the snakes. Shake up the notion that they
were there all along, alongside the orchards
plump with apples, perfect and round.
Then I'd tell them, Stay calm. There
is a God, but He's not a life coach. He's
not there to keep your kids from killing
each other, and He didn't need a snake
to tempt you. Hunger would have done
that in the end. Enjoy Him now, before
it all fans out to seven billion people and things
get so bad that He's afraid to come down
from the sky.

The Original Adam and Eve

ADAPTED BY STEVE ZEITLIN FROM A STORY IN HOWARD SCHWARTZ'S *TREE OF SOULS*[7]

Sir James George Frazer, the brilliant and often discredited Scottish mythologist,
suggested that the original story of Adam and Eve,
set down generations before Genesis,
was likely based, as early myths so often were, on polarities:
heaven and earth, day and night, sun and moon.

So before the Tree of Knowledge came into the picture,
Frazer speculates, the original Garden of Eden held two trees,

the Tree of Life and the Tree of Death,

created by God so Adam and Eve could choose

to be mortal or immortal.

God wished his creatures to be immortal,
gave them a surefire hint,
bellowed forth from above the trees of Eden,

Do not eat from the Tree of Death,
or
from this Garden, I will tear you both asunder.

But since God created contrarians,
they chose
the Tree of Death,
and so fell prey to their first mortal blunder.

> COMMENTARY: In the last words attributed to Moses in the Torah,
> this prophet of prophets looks into the soul of the Jewish people and
> implores them to choose life. Yet as fate would have it, in the above
> story Adam and Eve eat from the Tree of Death. Given a choice—that
> is, as soon as choice becomes an option and a privilege—people are
> apt to make the wrong one. We humans seem to have a gift for mak-
> ing the wrong decisions. In this earliest instance, we didn't even know
> to choose life—that is, eternal life. Then again, thinking about all that
> would entail, perhaps it was the right choice. (Flash Rosenberg)

COMMENTARY: Memory is what makes us human. Although memory is not referenced in Genesis, I conceive of memory as God's gift to humankind, beginning with Adam and Eve. We are continually ripped from our pasts as surely as Adam and Eve were banished from the Garden, and memory is what makes our lives meaningful. We validate and pass on our memories, enshrining them in stories, and their telling helps us remember. We don't know the value of a moment until it becomes a memory. Memory is a tool for the creation of meaning—God's gift to humankind as much so as the creation of the world. (Steve Zeitlin)

One of my favorite quotes regarding memory was written by the cognitive psychologist Roger Schank: "We need to tell someone else a story that describes our experiences because the process of creating the story also creates the memory structure that will contain the gist of the story for the rest of our lives. Talking is remembering."[8]

Talking also sets the story in the heart. By "heart," I mean the deep place in each of us with bridges to the feelings, connections, sense memories, and secrets we keep in our memories. According to the Torah, the Talmud, and folklore, the heart is not only the seat of wisdom but the seat of memory and recollection.

Interestingly, the word *ear* is embedded in the words *hear* and *heart*. Thus, we tell stories with the voice from the heart to reach the ears and hearts of others. Telling stories is essentially sharing from one heart to another. (Peninnah Schram)

The Birth of Memory

BY STEVE ZEITLIN

Banished from the garden, Adam cursed
God, Eden, his own rib, and the apple
Eve had eaten.
He held
her hand too tight as he walked
into the darkness of whatever was to be.

Then Eve turned
for a last glance at the garden.

Her glimpse unhardened
heaven's heart. God worried
death and time are too unkind,
and so graced
both Adam and Eve
with memory.

Enough!

CONTEMPORARY TALE RETOLD BY RABBI EDWARD SCHECTER

It is said that when Abraham
stood on the mountaintop
and raised his knife
to sacrifice Isaac,

it was not God
but Abraham's wife, Sarah,
who intervened,
stayed the knife,
cried,

Enough already!

COMMENTARY: That's a good one, because "enough already," *genug shoyn* in Yiddish, is like what your wife says. Leo Rosten's *The Joys of Yiddish* identifies "enough already" as one of the many Yiddish expressions that have infiltrated American English in translation.[9] (Zev Shanken)

The Razbash Describes God's Test

BY ZEV SHANKEN

God put Abraham to the test . . . said, "Take your son, your favored one, Isaac, whom you love, and go to the land of Moriah and offer him there as a burnt offering on one of the heights that I will point out to you." So early the next morning Abraham saddled his ass and took with him two servants and his son Isaac . . . (Gen. 22:2–3)

Here is the unrecorded exchange of what actually happened.

> *Here I am, O Lord,*
> *dagger in hand, poised to follow your instructions with zeal.*
> *But I must have answers, lest I disobey.*
> *Do I burn Isaac naked or with clothes?*
> *Do I sprinkle, drain, pour, or throw his blood on the pyre?*
> *Do I burn him up completely or share him with my family?*
> *Does hair count as fur?*
> *And since the place you have shown me is the future Temple Mount,*
> *should I sweep the ashes into the future Dung Gate,*
> *as is instructed for a sacrifice?*
>
> *Abraham, Abraham,* God says. *Do not sacrifice your son.*
> *For now I see how seriously you take Judaism.*

COMMENTARY: In my view, Judaism sometimes takes ritual, literalism, and hairsplitting legalism too far. By having Abraham ask technical questions based on actual sacrificial procedures outlined in Leviticus, this poem pokes fun at process-centered theology. Abraham gets God at the Divine's own game by asking absurdly technical questions—all derived from real sources. God, like a vaudeville straight man who knows better, plays along, revoking the commandment to sacrifice Isaac and saying, "For now I see how seriously you take Judaism." Seriously? (Zev Shanken)

The Prophet

TRADITIONAL TALE RETOLD BY RABBI EDWARD SCHECTER

A young prophet walks through the savage streets
of Sodom and Gomorrah, trumpets,
Be good, be kind, be generous.

A man approaches him.
Are you deranged?
Can't you see? These evil souls
will never change!

But I am not crying out in the hope that they will change,
replies the prophet.

I am crying out to be sure
that they
do not
change me.

Moses and the Superhero

BY FOLKLORIST JACK SANTINO

I imagine that Jerry Siegel and Joe Shuster,
high school students from Cleveland, Ohio,
knew all about Moses—

how his mother sent him away in a basket
when all the Hebrew boys were slated to be drowned
in the river Nile
and Pharaoh's daughter discovered him in the bulrushes.

Raised by Egyptians,
he became the hero of the Jewish people.

So Jerry and Joe named their child survivor
Kal-El
(in Hebrew, "All That Is God"),
imagined he was born
to distinguished parents on Krypton,
a planet soon destined to blow—
so they sent him to safety in a rocket ship.

Raised by farmers in Iowa,
Superman became the hero of Metropolis.

COMMENTARY: In the comics of 1938, Jerry Siegel and Joe
Shuster made Superman the ultimate immigrant: the hero who
had to "pass" as Clark Kent, the WASP, with a costume always
under his suit—the superhero the rest of the world doesn't see.
(Jack Santino)

113

COMMENTARY: Rabbi Hayim ben Joseph Vital's crazy dream seems rooted in the traditional idea, which emerged in the late Second Temple period, that God dictated the first five books of the Bible to Moses. As such, Moses, the central character in the Torah, came to be seen not only as the mediator of law but as the author of both the Torah's laws and its narrative. On another level, this reminds me of a song my wife and I once wrote, "You Are What You Love." When something is beautiful and meaningful to you, as the Torah was to Moses, you want to make it a part of you. Rabbi Vital imagines that Moses loved the sacred texts so deeply that, for a while, he and the Torah became one. (Steve Zeitlin)

Rabbi Hayim Vital Dreams of Moses

ADAPTED BY STEVE ZEITLIN FROM A TRADITIONAL TALE
IN HOWARD SCHWARTZ'S *TREE OF SOULS*[10]

Some say Moses received only the tablets on Mount Sinai,
others that the entire Torah was received that day.

Prophets say Moses memorized the Torah,
sent by God that day;
others that the Torah was internalized,
for Rabbi Vital dreamed
that when Moses passed away,
the ancient Rabbis laid him out on a long, wide table
and he transformed into a Torah scroll—
as they turned the corpse, the text unrolled.

Beginning with "In the beginning,"
the Rabbis around the table read
from Genesis to Deuteronomy.

Then Moses became Moses once again,
and when the Rabbi awoke,
he sensed the presence of the prophet in the room.

COMMENTARY: Miriam, the sister of Aaron and Moses, is called "Miriam the prophetess" (Miriam *Hanavia*). While she had only one prophecy, she deserves this honored title because this was a major prophecy.

A pharaoh arose in Egypt who feared that the Israelites were becoming too numerous. He ordered the Egyptian midwives to drown in the Nile all male babies born to the Jews. Miriam's father, Amram, and mother, Yocheved, decided to divorce so they would not have any more children and thus avoid having a son who would be killed. All the other Israelites came to the same conclusion. At that moment, Miriam had a prophecy that an Israelite leader would soon be born and lead the people out of Egypt. When she heard about her parents' plan, she challenged her father: "You are doing worse than Pharaoh—he ordered that boy babies be killed. But by divorcing, no Jewish children will be born—not boys and not girls. That will be the end of the Jewish people." Amram recognized his daughter's wisdom. So it is written, "A certain man of the house of Levi [Amram] went and married a Levite woman [Yocheved]. The woman conceived and bore a son . . ." (Exod. 2:1–2). This son was Moses, who became the leader of the Israelites and took them out of Egypt.

What a prophecy that was! Miriam had the merit to be given the well of fresh water that traveled with the Israelites as they wandered through the desert. (Peninnah Schram)

Miriam's Wandering Well

ADAPTED BY STEVE ZEITLIN FROM A TRADITIONAL TALE[11]

The sages from the days of Talmud tell
of the wandering freshwater well
that appeared and reappeared
before Miriam
to quench the thirst of desert Jews in their delirium.
They called it Miriam's well.

We modern Jews, too, need her well—
we adorn our seder tables
with Miriam's cup,
symbol of all that sustains us,

and when all is lost,
the poets, I've heard tell,
seek inspiration
from the wellspring of Miriam's wandering well.

Lamb's Blood

BY STEVE ZEITLIN

The Jews have seen it all:
the waters of the Nile turned blood red
frogs
lice
flies
pestilence
boils
hail
locusts
darkness
and the killing of the firstborn child.

But now
the world is quarantined
as if an *X* in lamb's blood
has been drawn upon our doors.

May this plague spare us all—
Christian, Hindu, Muslim, Jew.

May the Angel of Death pass over our houses.
May the Red Sea part.
May cities and towns reopen.
May we all pass through.

COMMENTARY: This poem comparing the COVID-19 pandemic to a biblical plague suggests that beyond following the guidance of trusted medical professionals, we can pray. Prayers aplenty can ground us as we confront a situation over which we have limited control. (Steve Zeitlin)

A Rabbinical Love Poem

BY ZEV SHANKEN

I used to think
that when the sages said,
The reward for a good deed, a mitzvah,
is the mitzvah,

they were cleverly ducking
the universal question:
What's my reward
for keeping the commandments?

But now I understand
that they understood love.
My reward for loving you
is that I get to love you.

COMMENTARY: The destructions of the First Temple (586 BCE) and the Second Temple (70 CE) loom large in Jewish thought and memory. Among the significant remains from the Second Temple period is the Western Wall, the retaining wall of the Temple Mount, also known as the Kotel, or the Wailing Wall. In Jewish mythology, this wall is also said to have remained from the First Temple, and to mark the spots both where God created the earth—the Foundation Stone—and where God told Jacob to sacrifice Isaac on Mount Moriah, the Altar of Abraham.[12] (Steve Zeitlin)

Twelve Rabbis Went to a Party

BY STORYTELLER, AUTHOR, AND PERFORMANCE
ARTIST ANNIE LANZILLOTTO

The second rabbi asked me a very strange question.
Strange in his soft intent listening: *How are you?*

*Geez, rabbi, thanks for asking. I'm poor, I'm sick, I'm alone,
I can't rest, and everyone I love is dead or far away.*

That's like the destruction of the First Temple, he said,
in 586 BCE. My name is Simkha. Come, talk to me.

Rabbi Simkha handed me a grid, the Complete Remedy
developed by Rabbi Nachman of Breslov, the great-grandson
of the founder of Hasidism, the mystic Baal Shem Tov.

#1. Sing a Psalm.
#2. Visit nature.
#3. Do something for someone in a worse situation than you.
#4. Contemplate the life of an ancestor or historical figure.

I practiced the grid. I walked around a big old pine tree
singing Psalm 118:

> *This is the day the Lord has made,
> let us rejoice and be glad. . . . Be glad, be glad. . . .*

I telephoned my elderly shut-in neighbor.
I contemplated the lives of my parents, grandparents,
great-grandparents, how they conquered terror,
struggled to survive.

I went back to Rabbi Simkha. *I'm still in a panic.*

Ahhh, it's like the destruction of the Second Temple, he said.

The Lamed Vavniks

BY PLAYWRIGHT AND THEATER DIRECTOR ARTHUR STRIMLING[13]

There is a Jewish tradition that in the whole world at any time,
there are 36 and only 36 wise and just people
who keep the world going.

They are called the Lamed Vavniks.
Now we don't necessarily know who they are,
in fact, they don't necessarily know who they are.

So anyone you meet, anyone you talk to,
perhaps the person sitting right next to you,
could be one of the 36.

COMMENTARY: The legend of the Lamed Vavniks is rooted in Hebrew numerology, which gives each letter a numerical value. *Lamed* equals thirty and *vav* equals six. Together, they total thirty-six, the number of righteous people who, in each generation, make the world possible. "Without their acts of lovingkindness," writes Rabbi Rami Shapiro, "life on this planet would implode under the weight of human selfishness, anger, ignorance and greed."[14] The legend is based, in part, on the tales of Sodom and Gomorrah in Genesis, in which God is willing to spare those cities for the sake of a few righteous souls. As God explains to Abraham, "I will spare the whole place for their sake."[15]

Author and *tzedakah* innovator Danny Siegel further observes that "there are [also] many, many more Second Level Righteous Ones. They are everywhere for us to see and work with, if we but open our eyes to seek them out."[16] (Steve Zeitlin)

6 JEWELS . . . *Shaped by the Holocaust*

DURING THE DEATH MARCH OF THE HOLOCAUST, JEWS NEVER STOPPED telling jokes and stories, writing poems, and staging plays as they tried to survive both mentally and physically, mostly in vain.

The Polish poet Tadeusz Różewicz wrote about creating poems "out of a remnant of words, salvaged words, out of uninteresting words, words from the great rubbish dump, the great cemetery."[1]

From her arrival at the Ravensbrück camp on October 21, 1943, until the fall of the camp in the spring of 1945, Germaine Tillion, a leader in the French resistance movement, penned a comic operetta, "Le verfügbar aux enfers" ("A camp worker goes to hell"), to entertain her fellow prisoners, writing it on the inside of a box guarded by her fellow inmates. The operetta, which depicted the camp life of the lowest class of prisoners, who could be used for any kind of work, was performed in Paris in 2007, more than sixty years later.[2]

Beginning when she was thirteen years old, Anne Frank kept a secret diary while she and her family were in hiding in a small room behind a fake bookcase in the building where her father, Otto Frank, worked. The Gestapo arrested the family in 1944, and Anne died in the Bergen-Belsen concentration camp. Otto Frank's secretary, Miep Gies, who had hidden the family, saved the diary. "That's the difficulty in these times," Anne had written. "Ideals, dreams, and cherished hopes rise within us, only to meet the horrible truth and be shattered. It's really a wonder that I haven't dropped all my ideals, because they seem so absurd and impossible to carry out. Yet I keep them, because in spite of everything I still believe that people are really good at heart."[3]

Holocaust survivor Renée Fodor Schwarz wrote with a twig in the sand outside the Auschwitz concentration camp barracks; she survived, but her work did not.

In his masterful collection of tales first published posthumously in 1815, Rabbi Nachman of Breslov says that when his great-grandfather the Baal Shem Tov saw that the lines of communication were severed and it was impossible to mend them with prayer, he restored contact by telling a tale.[4] Arising out of the devastating horror of the camps, the following poetic tales, stories, and poems are a testament to the resilience of the human spirit when confronted by the atrocity that a portion of humanity proved capable of executing.

Tickling the Corpse

BY STEVE ZEITLIN

To laugh is to imagine a world
in which the Holocaust never happened.

The Nazis killed the children first,
but amid the carnage of the Warsaw ghetto,
Jewish children were seen
playing among the limbs of the dead,
leaping over bodies,

playfully
tickling a corpse,

and sixty years later,
though we're tickling our Jewish souls,
laughter remains an act of faith.

Holocaust Jokes

CONTEMPORARY JOKE RETOLD BY ZEV SHANKEN

A comedian dies and goes to heaven.
He meets God and says,
Are you okay with Holocaust jokes?

God says, *Try me.*
The comedian tells God the joke.
God says, *I don't get it.*

The comedian replies,
Well, I guess you had to be there.

It Is Raining on the House of Anne Frank

BY POET LINDA PASTAN[5]

It is raining on the house
of Anne Frank
and on the tourists
herded together under the shadow
of their umbrellas,
on the perfectly silent
tourists who would rather be
somewhere else
but who wait here on stairs
so steep they must rise
to some occasion
high in the empty loft,
in the quaint toilet,
in the skeleton
of a kitchen
or on the map—
each of its arrows
a barb of wire—
with all the dates, the expulsions,
the forbidding shapes
of continents.
And across Amsterdam it is raining
on the Van Gogh Museum
where we will hurry next
to see how someone else
could find the pure
center of light
within the dark circle
of his demons.

COMMENTARY: Roslyn Bresnick-Perry says that she and her cousin Zisl were constant companions, but not because they particularly liked each other. "In fact, there were times when we actually hated each other. But since we lived next door . . . , had the same relatives, played the same games, liked getting into the same kind of trouble, we had no other recourse than to spend every possible moment together. Zisl was the one with the ideas, and I was always the willing follower."[7] For Roslyn, Zisl's loss was an unforgettable tragedy. As a storyteller, she went on to tell many tales of Zisl. These were especially close to her heart. (Peninnah Schram)

Riding with the Moon

ADAPTED BY STEVE ZEITLIN FROM A TRUE
STORY BY ROSLYN BRESNICK-PERRY[6]

One night in my village in Belarus,
I saw my aunt Faygele secretly kissing her beau.

One whisper to my mischievous cousin Zisl,
and she said: *Let's blackmail them*
into giving us a ride
aboard his beautiful horse-drawn sleigh.

I demanded the ride—but then Faygele
announced their engagement, stealing our thunder.

One night just before I left for America,
Faygele and her beau appeared in my bedroom
and, to my surprise,
whisked me away for the promised ride.

Years later, I still remember
how magically the sleigh glided over the snow,
the tinkling of the bell,
riding with the moon under a dark blue sky—

then my utter panic!
I'd forgotten to blow our secret whistle,
the one I used to wake up Zisl,
who'd contrived our moonlit ride.

My mother and I sailed for America.
Zisl, my mischievous cousin, ingenious friend,
perished in the Holocaust.

In the sleigh, dozing off that night,
I dreamed I was gliding to the moon,
where a round cage of icicles
had trapped Zisl,
sealing her in.

COMMENTARY: Krakow ghetto rebel Dolek Liebeskind is credited with these lines (shown in italics), which became a rallying cry on Friday, November 20, 1942, at the rebels' dinner to "greet the Sabbath bride." The rebels, Dolek insisted, would fight for the sake of "three lines in history," if only to show that "Jewish youth did not go like sheep to the slaughter." The group named this occasion "The Last Supper," recognizing there was not much chance all of them would survive—they were greeting the Sabbath as a group for the last time. Subsequently discovered in his hideout, Dolek chose to die while exchanging gunfire rather than allow himself to be captured. A fellow rebel, Yehuda Poldek-Maimon, was captured and transferred to Auschwitz. He survived to tell the story. In *To Bear Witness: Holocaust Remembrance at Yad Vashem*, Yehuda reflects on that Sabbath evening: "It was an unforgettable night. We felt for the first time since the outbreak of the war that we regained our status as human beings."[9] (Steve Zeitlin)

Last Supper in the Krakow Ghetto

ADAPTED BY STEVE ZEITLIN FROM ORAL TESTIMONIES BY
SURVIVORS OF THE KRAKOW GHETTO UPRISING[8]

At the last Sabbath
in the final days of the Krakow ghetto rebellion,
Dolek Liebeskind says,
This is the last time we'll meet.

We are on the road to death.
If you want life, don't look for it here.
We are at the end of days.

In the ghettos of Vilna, Minsk, Bialystok, and Krakow,
the defiant courage of the rebels
grows stronger as their strength depletes.

In Warsaw, the bodies will never be found
beneath the debris of rebel headquarters on Mila Street.

We didn't set out to win a victory, Dolek says.
Victory isn't ours to win.

Let us say we fought and died
for three lines in Jewish history.

Hovering above the Pit

ADAPTED BY STEVE ZEITLIN FROM A TALE RETOLD
BY JUDAIC SCHOLAR YAFFA ELIACH[10]

Rabbi Manasseh ben Israel and his friend, an atheist,
stood at the edge of a pit in Auschwitz
with nowhere to run to or hide.

My friend, said the rabbi, *man must follow the will of God.*
If it was ordained that pits be dug
and we are commanded to jump,
then pits will be shoveled,
and jump we must.

As the command was given, and the gunfire began,
the rabbi whispered, *We will jump.*

When they opened their eyes, they found themselves
standing on the other side of the pit,
escaping through a hole in the fence.

For your sake, Rabbi, I am still alive.
Tell me: How did you get through?

I was holding on to my ancestral merit, Abraham, Isaac, and Jacob.
I was holding on to the coattails of my father and grandfather of blessed memory
when I flew.

Tell me, my friend, the rabbi asked, *how did* you *reach the other side?*

I was holding on to you.

COMMENTARY: This poem, along with "Hovering above the Pit," derive from Yaffa Eliach's marvelous book, *Hasidic Tales of the Holocaust*. Eliach herself first heard many of these stories at the home of Holocaust survivor Rabbi Israel Spira in 1975. The tales manifest metaphysical resistance to the Holocaust: the ability to maintain unfettered belief in the face of desolation and destruction. They are filled with the stench of barracks and the feel of barbed wire, but they are set in the human heart. (Steve Zeitlin)

In the Janowska Street Ghetto

ADAPTED BY MARC KAMINSKY FROM A STORY RETOLD BY YAFFA ELIACH[11]

A woman pale as a sheet,
eyes burning with a strange
fire, walked
with the others to the Umschlagplatz.

Halt!
called the German guard,
machine gun trained on the prisoners,

whereupon she glimpsed the knife protruding
from the top pocket of his uniform.

Hand me that knife, she demanded.
Taken by surprise, he did.

She bent down and picked up
what looked like a bundle of rags at her feet.
With steady hands, she opened
the knife, unwound a long white sheet,

and with one smooth stroke,
she circumcised her newborn son.

She straightened her back, looked up
to the heavens, and said, *God,*
You gave me a healthy child. I'm returning
to You a wholesome kosher Jew.

And she handed her baby to the guard
in his receiving blanket and shroud.

COMMENTARY: The second youngest of ten children born in a village near Krakow, Poland, Renée Fodor Schwarz became orphaned at age four. Despite having older siblings, she had to mother herself—with determination and grit. She enrolled at Jagiellonian University in Krakow, buoyed by the dream of studying psychoanalysis with Sigmund Freud—a dream that abruptly ended when the Nazis invaded Poland. Imprisoned first in the Krakow ghetto and then at the Auschwitz concentration camp, she managed to escape during a death march near the end of the war. She moved to Israel, then to the United States, and went on to have a successful career in psychology. (Steve Zeitlin)

The Twig

ADAPTED BY STEVE ZEITLIN FROM RENÉE
FODOR SCHWARZ'S MEMOIR *RENÉE*[12]

At Auschwitz, pens, pencils, and writing paper were forbidden.
Yet before sunset one day,
I remained outside the barracks
and cleared a space in the sand till it felt smooth as paper.

With a twig, I started to write,
while the others, fearful, avoided watching.
When I was done, I carefully covered my writing with sand.

As I erased, I tried to recall what I'd written,
but the fear of being caught made it impossible.

So many parts of me were lost in the war.
This precious one I left in the sand.

In Memory of Those Who Died in Vain in the Holocaust

EXCERPTED FROM A POEM BY RENÉE FODOR SCHWARZ[13]

In memory of all those who were sentenced to death without a reason.

In memory of all those who were killed before they began life's
journey . . .

In memory of mothers who chose to die with their children rather than
leave them.

In memory of mothers who never stopped crying for their lost children.

In memory of fathers who could not protect their families from death.

In memory of the young who watched their parents be shot and were
powerless to save their lives.

In memory of those who had to watch their loved ones die by hanging.

In memory of those who had to bury their brothers and sisters in mass
graves.

In memory of those who died while trying to save the life of a loved one.

In memory of those who never left their families and who died together.

In memory of those who tried to save their lives and failed.

In memory of those who tried to help but did not succeed . . .

In memory of those who forgot their names and instead remembered
the numbers tattooed on their arm . . .

In memory of those who, still alive, walked in hell.

In memory of those who, stripped naked, were shot.

In memory of those who were thirsty but had no water to drink.

In memory of those who had no shoes to wear.

In memory of those who had false hopes.

In memory of those who did not want to die . . .

In memory of those who set wedding dates which they could not
keep . . .

In memory of those who, burning with fever, had no one to put a wet
cloth on their forehead . . .

In memory of those who had no human rights . . .

Forgotten Acts of Courage

ADAPTED BY STEVE ZEITLIN AND MARC KAMINSKY FROM
ALEX BORSTEIN'S EMMY ACCEPTANCE SPEECH[14]

Some say Jews went to their deaths
like sheep to the slaughter,
but many acts of courage were buried
when the witnesses were gunned down.

As she accepted an Emmy Award for
The Marvelous Mrs. Maisel,
Alex Borstein told the story of her grandmother
who stood in line
to be shot at the edge of a pit.

She asked the guard, *What happens*
if I step out of line?
The guard said, *I don't have the heart*
to kill you—but somebody will.

So she stepped out of line,
Alex said, *and for that,*
I am here,
and for that, my children are here.

So step out of line, ladies.
Step out of line.

COMMENTARY: According to Jewish tradition, we each have three names: the name given to us, the name that others give us, and the name we give (or make) for ourselves (see Eccles. Rabbah 7:3; Tanhumah Vayakhel 1; Midrash Shmuel 23). Ashkenazic Jews often name their children after someone in the family who has died, as a way of keeping that person alive in their memories and in the family history; Sephardic Jews also name a child after a beloved person who is still alive. Other times, Jews will name a child after an esteemed biblical character or a respected individual or personal hero, hoping that the child will grow into the name and develop that person's characteristics. In this story-poem, there are a number of people named Rachel in whose honor the baby girl is named, with the hope that she will carry on their stories.

In one verse, the name Rachel is chosen to remember the Rachel in Torah (Gen. 29–35), who becomes the beloved wife of Jacob. It's a beautiful love story! A wonderful rendering of this tale can be found in the poem and song "Zemer Nuge" ("A Melancholic Song"), which has become a classic in Israel. The Israeli poet known as Rachel waits to be reunited with her love and compares it with the time that the biblical Rachel waited to be reunited with Jacob. (Peninnah Schram)

Rachel

(Rachel [rā' chal], a ewe)

BY LINDA PASTAN[15]

We named you
for the sake
of the syllables
and for the small boat
that followed the *Pequod*,
gathering the lost children
of the sea.

We named you
for the dark-eyed girl
who waited at the well
while her lover
worked seven years
and again
seven.

We named you
for the small daughters
of the Holocaust
who followed their six-pointed stars
to death,
and were all of them
known as
Rachel.

COMMENTARY: André Schwartz-Bart's 1959 novel *Le dernier des justes* (*The Last of the Just*), traces the story of one Jewish family from the time of the Crusades to the gas chambers of Auschwitz. This scene takes place on the train to Auschwitz. In his book *Waiting for the Last Bus*, the writer Richard Holloway also quotes this passage, describing Bart's novel as one of the great books of the twentieth century and wisely concluding: "It turns out that there are times when it is impossible to accept the utter finality of death. A child's death is one of them. *There is no room for truth here.* There is only room for the impossible act of consolation."[17] (Steve Zeitlin)

Death Train

LINED OUT FROM ANDRÉ SCHWARTZ-BART'S *THE LAST OF THE JUST*[16]

On the death train to Auschwitz,
a child died in Ernie's arms.

He's my brother, a little girl said hesitantly, anxiously . . .

He sat down next to her and set her on his knees.
He'll wake up too, in a little while, with all the others,
When we reach the Kingdom of Israel.
There children can find their parents, and everybody is happy.
Because the country we're going to, that's our Kingdom, know it well. . . .

There, a child interrupted happily . . .
There, we will be warm day and night . . .

There, said a second voice in the gloom,
There are no Germans or railway-cars
or anything that hurts. . . .

A woman digs her fingernails into Ernie's shoulder . . .
How can you tell them it's only a dream? she breathed,
with hate in her voice.

Rocking the child mechanically, Ernie gave way to dry sobs.
Madame, he said finally, *there is no room for truth here.*

Kaddish in the Boxcar of Death

BY YIDDISH POET AARON ZEITLIN, TRANSLATED FROM
THE YIDDISH BY MORRIS M. FAIERSTEIN[18]

In a sealed boxcar of death,
wrapped in barbed wire,
a Jew stands up and talks to God.
I'm carrying candles. You see? I am lighting them.
All of us in this car
will recite Kaddish
for ourselves. Glorified and Sanctified
is His Great Name.

Without tears,
everyone recited the Kaddish for himself or herself—
and God began
to recite Kaddish for the world.

COMMENTARY: Kaddish (the mourner's prayer) is often chanted for eleven months after the death of a parent, and in some communities for thirty days after the death of a spouse, sibling, or child. Some Jewish parents even refer to their oldest child as their "Kaddish," for these children are the ones who will mourn the parents following their deaths. It is unusual, if not sacrilegious, for Aaron Zeitlin to refer to the Jews in the boxcar of death as chanting Kaddish for themselves. However, he knows that many of the parents and grandparents—whom these Jews would have said Kaddish for someday—and many of their children, who would have said Kaddish for them, will also perish in the Holocaust. Their prayers, and the beautiful image of God saying Kaddish for the world, are fully justified. (Steve Zeitlin)

Face in the Mirror

ADAPTED BY STEVE ZEITLIN FROM A TRUE STORY OF HOLOCAUST
SURVIVOR BORIS BLUM, RETOLD BY HIS DAUGHTER TOBY BLUM-DOBKIN

Packed into the parlor of a German mansion
following the liberation of the camps,
Blum saw a mirror on the wall.
But among all the straggling skeletons,
he could not recognize his own reflection.
So he stuck out his tongue,
made funny faces,

and, years later, recognized traces of himself
in the story.
Mirror of memory,

pieced together from shards

of shattered silence.

JEWels . . . in Glimpses of Jewish American Lives

POET EMMA LAZARUS (1849–87) IS PERHAPS BEST KNOWN FOR "THE New Colossus," a sonnet she penned and donated to an auction to raise funds for the building of the Statue of Liberty; by 1903 it would be inscribed on a bronze plaque on the statue's pedestal. Her famous lines from "The New Colossus" would then welcome, among others, the largest group of Jewish immigrants to America arriving at New York's Ellis Island, beginning in the 1880s and ending in the 1920s:

> *"Keep, ancient lands, your storied pomp!" cries she*
> *With silent lips. "Give me your tired, your poor,*
> *Your huddled masses yearning to breathe free,*
> *The wretched refuse of your teeming shore.*
> *Send these, the homeless, tempest-tost to me,*
> *I lift my lamp beside the golden door!"*

Lazarus's own ancestors were some of the original twenty-three Portuguese Jews who first settled in the United States. These twenty-three beleaguered Jewish men, women, and children from Recife, Brazil, had arrived in New Amsterdam (later New York) in 1654, fleeing the Inquisition that was coming for them once the Portuguese took control of Recife from the Dutch.

And so it is that these famous lines speak, among other things, to the long-standing presence of Jews in America.

For the German Jews who came to America fleeing famine (1840–60), the Jews of Eastern Europe who escaped from pogroms (1880–1920), the survivors of the Holocaust (1945–50), and the Jews who fled the Soviet Union (1978–90), among others, America was a promised land. It is said that one such immigrant, induced by tales of America's gold-paved streets, arrived only to discover that none of the streets were paved with gold, some weren't paved at all—and he was the one who would have to pave them. America was a land of contradictory realities. Jews encountered dire poverty, overcrowding, and antisemitism as well as opportunities to earn PhDs, start businesses, and strike it rich. American Jews could choose to flaunt or downplay their Jewishness—or both—depending on what the situation required.

While there is no way to simplify the American Jewish experience for those immigrants and the Jews who succeeded them, the stories that follow embody some of its innumerable truths.

Rummage

BY MARC KAMINSKY[1]

I love the poorer sort
of antiques shops
that are really collections of junk:
a pair of spectacles
through which living eyes
once mastered the essentials of English,
a spindle
whose first cousin
might have been whispered to
by Morris Rosenfeld
in his shop on Eldridge Street,
a comb
that accompanied a recently buried widow
across the Atlantic,
a gift from her mother
at the time of marriage—
objects whose one value
is that they were cherished
by imaginary kin,
in them I trace
a saga of immigration
to a world that's no longer fresh
and feel
the etherealizing power
of long usage
which transforms small things
truly needed
into relics.

COMMENTARY: When my grandmother emigrated from Russia in the early twentieth century, the only object of value she carried—and eventually handed down to her daughters—was a samovar, a Russian invention of the mid-eighteenth century that is appreciated as an art object today. Its journey rendered it a precious heirloom and a symbol of my family's Jewish life in the old country. It also became emblematic of suburban American life when my aunt Mitzi converted it into a lamp. (Steve Zeitlin)

My most novel possession from the Old Country is a dress made from the Tzarina Alexandra's gown.

It came to us care of an uncle who was drafted into the Russian army during the Russian Revolution while the family was living in Belarus (White Russia). As Tzar Nicholas and his wife, the Tzarina Alexandra, were being overthrown, they tried to ferry their possessions on trains to safety, but Russian soldiers, including my uncle, boarded the trains and looted the contents. My uncle somehow got his hands on a magnificent ball gown, which he brought to his mother.

How to describe pure beauty? Silk—gossamer with a grayish background—is lined with a thicker silk. A variety of leaves interplay on the background—some five petals like a palm leaf, others a triangular leaf with half of the threads turquoise and the other half silver. Those turquoise threads become other blues when bathed in light.

Out of this one gown was enough material for three dresses. My grandmother had a dressmaker make dresses for herself, my mother, and her other daughter. My mother would wear her "Tzarina's dress," tailored with very thin lapels and a slightly flared skirt, every year on the High Holidays at the shul where my father was the *hazzan*. I would sit with my mother in the balcony of our Orthodox synagogue in New London, Connecticut, as she inhabited that dress with dignity and pleasure.

The saga of this dress is linked with my mother's story of leaving her homeland in White Russia for America. She finally arrived in 1926, after being stuck for three years in Cherbourg because of the U.S. immigration quota, and in her luggage was the Tzarina's gown.

Today, it is the only one of the three dresses to survive. It hangs in my closet in a clothes bag awaiting being passed on to my daughter. I've never tried it on. In this way I hold on to a treasured image of my mother in the Tzarina's dress that she always felt royal wearing. (Peninnah Schram)

Yiddishe Mama during World War II

LINED OUT FROM THE ESSAY "THE HEALING POWER OF JOKES"
BY PSYCHOTHERAPIST ALTER YISRAEL SHIMON FEUERMAN[2]

My father told me the following joke, which he swore was true:
A boy from the Bronx found himself fighting for Patton in the Battle of
   the Bulge.
In the frozen foxhole he wrote a letter to his mother back home.

*The bombs and the bullets are flying, the shells are exploding next to us
   from the air.*
An 88mm shell landed on the foxhole next to mine,
three men were blown to hell,
and the man next to me lost an arm.

The mother replied: *Hershel, I am sending you a salami, but I am
   warning you:*
*Whatever is going between Patton and the Germans, however bad it gets,
   stay out of it.*
Don't get involved.

It has nothing what to do with you!

COMMENTARY: This reminds me of an anecdote that I believe the
cartoonist Jules Feiffer related in his autobiography, *Backing into
Forward*. In 1945, right after the first atomic bomb was dropped
on Hiroshima, sixteen-year-old Jules rushed to his mother.
"Mom," he said, "do you realize what just happened? They cre-
ated a bomb that could destroy the world!" His mother's response
to this news? "Great, that's all I need right now." (Bob Mankoff)

Plucking the Chicken

ADAPTED BY STEVE ZEITLIN FROM A TRADITIONAL
JOKE RETOLD BY ABE LASS

Abe Lass
remembers the live chicken market on the Lower East Side
from when he was a boy.

There is Mrs. Cohen, the customer.
Mr. Schwartz, the butcher.
And dozens of squawking chickens.

Schwartz is convinced Mrs. Cohen is stealing the live chickens.
She's wearing an oversize coat in the midst of summer
He can almost spot her shoving a chicken in there.

Every day Schwartz counts the chickens
and cries, *Foul!*

At last he confronts her:

Mrs. Cohen, you have just stolen a chicken.

No, I have not, Mr. Schwartz!

So he lifts his arm,
reaches for the top of her coat,
and flicks his hand in.

A look of surprise overtakes his face.

So quick you plucked the chicken?

Getting Dressed

BY STEVE ZEITLIN

In front of the mirror in the house on Drexel Road in West Philly,
Grandpop Harry taught me
how to tie a tie;
Uncle Jay, how to fold a sports coat.

My father, Irving, taught me
that a shirt has four corners.
My mother, Shirley, said to hold on to my cuffs
when putting on a sweater.

Underneath our clothes,
Uncle Adolph used to say,
we are all naked.

I wear them all each day,
naked, fully clothed.

No More Birthdays

BY THE FIRST POET LAUREATE OF QUEENS, NEW YORK, HAL SIROWITZ[3]

Don't swing the umbrella in the store,
Mother said. There are all these glass jars
of spaghetti sauce above your head
that can fall on you, & you can die.
Then you won't be able to go to tonight's party,
or go to the bowling alley tomorrow.
And instead of celebrating your birthday
with soda & cake, we'll have
anniversaries of your death with tea
& crackers. And your father and I won't
be able to eat spaghetti anymore, because
the marinara sauce will remind us of you.

A Short History of Judaic Thought
in the Twentieth Century

BY LINDA PASTAN[4]

The rabbis wrote:
although it is forbidden
to touch a dying person,
nevertheless, if the house
catches fire
he must be removed
from the house.

Barbaric!
I say,
and whom may I touch then
aren't we all
dying?

You smile
your old negotiator's smile
and ask:
but aren't all our houses
burning?

At a Bungalow in the Rockaways

TRADITIONAL JOKE

Four women play mah-jongg in hushed silence.
No sound but the clicking of tiles.

The first one can't sustain the quiet: *Oy.*

The second can't help herself: *Oy vey.*

The third gives in: *Oy, veis meir.*

Okay, says the fourth,
I thought we weren't going to talk about our children.

Tradition!

TRADITIONAL JOKE

The new rabbi was despondent.
At every service, when a particular prayer was said,
half the congregation stood while the other half sat,
and those who stood yelled at the ones who sat,
and those who sat yelled at the ones who stood,
and no one could hear the prayers.

The question of the authentic synagogue tradition needed to be resolved.

The rabbi finally tracked down a hundred-year-old former congregant.
But before he could say anything,
both the sitters and the standers had encircled him.

In the beginning, we all sat, right? one sitter asked.

No, said the old man.

That's right! said a stander.
We all stood for the prayer.
That *was the correct position.*

That's not right, either, said the old man.

See? explained the rabbi. *This is the problem:*
The sitters yell at those who stand,
and the standers yell at those who sit.

That's it! said the old man.
That was the tradition!

> COMMENTARY: At one synagogue I know of, the men walked
> proudly around the entire synagogue whenever they were going
> to read from the Torah, or whenever they were returning the
> Torah to the Ark, among other times, and whenever they got to
> a certain spot, they bowed. Someone asked the rabbi why they

bowed at that place in their procession, and he said, "I don't know. We'll have to ask the rabbi who was here before me." When they asked that rabbi, he also answered, "I don't know. We'll have to ask the rabbi before me." So the committee went to the nursing home, where a very elderly rabbi listened to the question and laughed. "Oh," he said, "when I was the rabbi there, at that very spot there was a hanging chandelier. And since it was hanging low, the men had to bend down to go under the lamp. When they removed that lamp, the men continued bowing out of habit."

Aha! So begins a tradition! (Peninnah Schram)

Jewish and Goyish

ADAPTED BY STEVE ZEITLIN FROM A ROUTINE
BY COMEDIAN LENNY BRUCE[5]

Dig: I'm Jewish.
Count Basie's Jewish.
Ray Charles is Jewish.

Eddie Cantor's goyish.
B'nai B'rith is goyish.
Hadassah, Jewish.

If you live in New York or any other big city, you are Jewish.
It doesn't matter even if you're Catholic;
if you live in New York, you're Jewish.

If you live in Butte, Montana,
you're going to be goyish
even if you're Jewish.

COMMENTARY: Fun fact: the first mayor of Butte, Montana—Henry Jacobs—was Jewish. (Bob Mankoff)

According to the *My Jewish Learning* website, Lenny Bruce (1925–66) "is something of a patron saint—make that rebbe—to American Jewish comedians. He's a hero and martyr to the cause."[6] Born Leonard Alfred Schneider, he was imprisoned on obscenity charges numerous times during his brief career, but he was never willing to censor his performances. The "Jewish and Goyish" joke can be seen as poking fun at the Jewish propensity to categorize everything in the world as either Jewish or non-Jewish. He can also be seen as honoring Jewish funk—that is, all things infused with a bit of urban irony, soul, or funk appear more Jewish in his universe. As he calls it, fruit salad, pumpernickel bread, black cherry soda, macaroons, and Italians are decidedly Jewish, but lime Jell-O, white bread, trailer parks, Drake's cakes, and Greeks are "goyish"—a term seen as denigrating today but that's still applicable to describe, say, a ham sandwich on white bread with mayonnaise. (Steve Zeitlin)

The Great Trick Is to Know Who You Are

LINED OUT FROM THE COMEDIAN JACKIE MASON'S ONE-
MAN BROADWAY SHOW *THE WORLD ACCORDING TO ME*

The great trick is to know who you are.
Most people don't know.
Thank God I know.

There was a time I didn't know.
I'm not ashamed to admit it.
I went to a psychiatrist. I did.
He took a look at me.
Right away he said, *This is not you.*
I said, *This is not me, then who is it?*
He said, *I don't know either.*
So I said, *Then what do I need you for?*
He said, *To find out who you are.*
He said, *Together, we're going to look for the real you.*
I said, *If I don't know who I am,*
then how do I know who to look for?
Besides, if I want to find me, why do I need him?. . . .

He said, *The search, the search for the real you*
will have to continue. That will be a hundred dollars, please.

COMMENTARY: Classic talmudic reasoning goes on steroids in this monologue from one of Jackie Mason's Broadway shows. A soul can experience vertigo trying to bend the mind around such convoluted logic. Appropriately, Mason brings this reasoning to bear on a visit to a psychiatrist, a figure that has often replaced the rabbi in American Jewish folklore. Mason also seems to draw upon the Yiddish saying *"Az ikh vel zayn vi er, ver vet zayn vi ikh?"*: "If I should be like someone else, who would be like me?" (Steve Zeitlin)

Skin Check

BY ESTHER COHEN

Peggy said everyone likes him so I went
to Dr. Adam Geyer of Tribeca Dermatology
for my first-ever skin check.

I'm in the "Oh no" category of too pale, too old
Ashkenazi Jews, and every day I see something
that wasn't there before,
google to see what it is, find
horrible pictures of flesh-eating possibilities.

Yesterday I went to check them all out with a
paid professional, Dr. Adam Geyer, Peggy's
favorite, and when he walked in, young and on time,
he said, *I'm Adam. Tell me everything that's
making you nervous now.*
Was I limited to skin? I asked.
Absolutely not, he said.

It Reminds Me of Those Old Jokes

TRADITIONAL JOKE[7]

Herbie walks into a psychiatrist's office, and tells him,
I can't stop snapping my fingers.

Why are you doing that? the psychiatrist asks.

To keep the elephants away.

But that's crazy—
there's no elephant within five thousand miles of here.

You see, it's working.

Hmmm, said the psychiatrist, *what else?*

It's my brother Abie.
He's gone crazy, crazy, crazy—
he thinks he's a chicken.

Doc says,
Why don't you bring him in so I can check him out?
I would—but I need the eggs.

COMMENTARY: On the one hand, it's a joke, but we infer meaning from it—we conclude, for instance, that life is a constellation of delusions—and we *need* them for our sanity. (Bob Mankoff)

The Rabbi

BY BARBARA KIRSHENBLATT-GIMBLETT

If you have to ask the Rabbi,
the answer is no.

Reflection

BY ZEV SHANKEN

Introducing me to his hospice nurse,
my dad pointed to me and said,
This is my son. I used to be him.

True Story

BY PUBLICIST CAROL KLENFNER

Grandpa, a child asks,
is the glass half-empty or half-full?

What does it matter? he answers.
It's such a beautiful glass.

COMMENTARY: If the glass is half-full, half-full with what? It all depends on what the glass is half-full of. The Razbash adds this reversal of the traditional parable: The kvetch says, "My glass is only half full." The tzadik says, "Thank God my glass is only half empty." (Zev Shanken)

To Kvell or Not to Kvell

ADAPTED BY STEVE ZEITLIN FROM A TRADITIONAL
JOKE RETOLD BY RABBI EDWARD SCHECTER

Sadie, said Shirley, *I'm just kvelling.*
My daughter is so, so lucky—she married a professor.

Shirley, that's wonderful.

But it didn't quite work out.

Oh no, said Sadie.

But then she married a doctor.

Oh my God! I can see why you're kvelling!

That didn't quite work out either, said Shirley.

I'm so sorry, said Sadie.

But then she married a lawyer.

Ah, Sadie said, *that's wonderful.*
Can you imagine, so much nachas
from just one daughter!

COMMENTARY: Both of these Americanized Yiddish words, *kvelling* and *nachas*, are jewels. *Kvelling* means "taking pride," and *nachas* is that pride, rightfully taken. While both expressions speak to the experience of deriving absolute delight from the accomplishments of others, most often *kvelling* and *nachas* are used in the context of parents exulting over their children. It's fair to say that nothing pleases Jewish parents more than *kvelling* over their kids' accomplishments—except, perhaps, deriving *nachas* from their friends for the same reason. (Steve Zeitlin)

The Free-Yarmulke Bin

BY STEVE ZEITLIN

Often when I headed to shul,
I forgot my yarmulke,
and on the way in,
took one from the free-yarmulke bin.

A closet in my house
grew full of those yarmulkes
that could not be thrown away.
Some were black, some gold, some lavender, some blue.
Some had been embroidered for special occasions—
   Abe Herman's bar mitzvah, 1962
   Rachel and David Cohen's wedding, 1973.
All were small and round, like my own soul, perhaps.

Last year, I carefully placed each one in a shopping bag
and, as I entered shul on Yom Kippur, preparing to atone,
placed them back in the free-yarmulke bin.

Would they circulate through other lives?
Or circle souls back home?

The Kiss

BY MARK SOLOMON[8]

My overturned yarmulke all there was between us. Desire pressed
   us into one another, whispered, "Yes!"—No Voice, no
      Person rose to challenge its demand. There was no freedom
   in the silence, the darkness. There was your mouth, full of matches, my
      rags of gasoline.

The Driver Said

BY ROBERT HERSHON[9]

boerum hill?
it used to be
gowanus
this ain't no
neighborhood
if ya butcher
comes to ya funeral
that's a
neighborhood

COMMENTARY: I've always loved Robert Hershon's poem because it provides a definition of *community*. A community is created when people know one another beyond a single interest, caring about one another in multiple ways. Jews have often struggled to balance being Jewish and being American. They've wanted to feel safe within their Jewish community even as they ventured outside it to "make it" in America. Even Jews who weren't religious, who'd never set foot in a synagogue, would choose to live fully around other Jews—someplace where the Jewish butcher they frequented would come to their funeral. (Steve Zeitlin)

COMMENTARY: Clara Lemlich Shavelson was a leader of the Uprising of 20,000, a strike of shirtwaist workers in New York's garment industry in 1909. Speaking in Yiddish, she told the crowd that she had something to say and they'd all better listen—and then she called for action. She was unstoppable and said so; she wouldn't rest until garment workers had fair working conditions. Because of her and many other organizers, the International Ladies' Garment Workers' Union formed and advocated for fair wages and better working conditions in sweatshops. At its peak in the 1920s and 1930s, the union had 450,000 members, mostly women, who understood the power of collective bargaining. Nowadays, every year, many organizations committed to labor rights—including Labor Arts, Remember the Triangle Fire Coalition, and Workers United (today's garment workers' union)—host the Clara Lemlich Awards at the Museum of the City of New York, celebrating women activists in their eighties and nineties who are still fighting to better the lives of working people. As a cofounder of the awards with Rachel Bernstein, I have been privileged to hear Clara's daughter, a fierce yet gentle woman named Rita Margules, tell Clara's amazing story each year. (Esther Cohen)

Clara

BY STEVE ZEITLIN

If I forget you, o Jerusalem,
may my right hand wither,
may my tongue forget its speech.

Clara Lemlich, a *fabrente meydl*—a fiery working girl
with flashing black eyes—
recalled that ancient oath from the psalms
when she demanded to *say a few words,*
rising to interrupt the speeches of the labor movement elders
in the Great Hall of Cooper Union
on November 22, 1909,

then led twenty thousand shirtwaist makers out to the picket line
to change the laws for working people—
an early union maid unfazed.
Her phrase—

If I turn traitor to the cause,
may my hand wither
from the arm I raise.

Alicia

BY STEVE ZEITLIN

Paper-thin baby-faced darling waif granddaughter
of traveling Jewish minstrels, *klezmorim,*

who fell in love with fiddles
and dated only Jewish girls,

klezbian meydlakh!

Your shtetl songs decipher death—
mournful tunes in the key of life—
your music, a bird's song, a threnody,
wafting over creation on a melody.

COMMENTARY: I wrote this poem after watching Alicia Svigals, among the world's premiere klezmer fiddlers, perform with the pioneering klezmer ensemble the Klezmatics. I shared it with Alicia, who was flattered, and we began a correspondence. "My grandfather Philip Svigals was a Jewish traveling minstrel of sorts," she told me. "He was a pianist who accompanied some of the greats: Judy Garland when she had her run at the Palace Theatre in New York, Sid Caesar on his TV shows *Your Show of Shows* and *Your Hit Parade*. He traveled all over the United States doing gigs, with his family in tow, so that my father never went to the same school for more than a few months as a child (which was hard on him). I didn't get to spend much time with my grandfather—he died when I was eleven—but he played music with me when I was little. Once, I wrote a melody and he arranged it for piano—I still wish I could find that!" (Steve Zeitlin)

Sally

ADAPTED BY STEVE ZEITLIN FROM A TRUE STORY TOLD
BY SALLY YARMOLINSKY'S FRIEND ANITA NAGER

Kneeling on the rumpled bed
on her last night on earth,
Sally Yarmolinsky,

comfortable in polka dots,
ruby lips, and big red hats.
Gloriously gaudy Sally—

her face a ghastly white—

unearthed
a tube of lipstick,
looked death in the mirror,
applied the color smooth and bright.

COMMENTARY: Sally Yarmolinsky (1949–2006), a doyenne of the New York City community arts world, encapsulated joie de vivre. Her friend Anita Nager told this story at her memorial. Another friend, Laura Hansen, told a story about how she and Sally once rescued some stone lions from a dumpster on the Upper East Side and lugged them back to Brooklyn. "She found joy in everything," Laura wrote. "She was adventurous and well-traveled, so had lots of opportunity to be enthralled by new things. She was an avid hiker and managed to be a decades-long member of the Appalachian Mountain Club without knowing how to drive. And she proudly did don polka dots and humongous hats." (Steve Zeitlin)

COMMENTARY: Assembling a minyan (a minimum of ten men) for an Orthodox service in the burned-out South Bronx in the 1970s and early 1980s was never easy. One morning, when only six men could be rounded up, one of the six observed that every person over age sixty-five gets two annual deductions from the Internal Revenue Service, and if the IRS counts each person twice, certainly God could do the same. On that particular occasion, he was overruled. (Steve Zeitlin)

Moishe Said

ADAPTED BY STEVE ZEITLIN FROM A STORY BY
ANTHROPOLOGIST JACK KUGELMASS[10]

Welcome aboard Noah's Ark, Moishe exclaimed.

Through the ice and snow of winter,
and the fires ravaging the neighborhood,
Moishe kept the last old synagogue in the South Bronx afloat,
each Sabbath hunting and gathering
ten men, African Jews, Marrano Jews, any soul
left in the South Bronx—
God, too, once stood in
for the tenth man.

One time, Mordechai and Rashim said they were done.
Mordechai couldn't worship with Rashim,
No, no! Rashim couldn't worship with Mordechai—

and that meant finis
for the last old synagogue in the South Bronx,
the soul home
of African Jews, Marrano Jews,
God too.

But Moishe, the peacemaker, found a way.

> *You know the guy who tries to break through ice*
> *on the sea in the middle of winter,*
> *chops and chops and chops*
> *but it still freezes over?*
> *If he waits till spring, the ice thaws.*

COMMENTARY: Descended from preeminent European rabbis, the theologian, philosopher, and activist Abraham Joshua Heschel was born in Warsaw in 1907. He escaped to the United States in 1940 but had to leave his family behind. His sister Esther was killed in a German bombing; his mother and two other sisters, Gittel and Devorah, were murdered by the Nazis.

In the United States, Heschel came to be considered the closest the country had produced to a Hebrew prophet—one fully committed to activism. He delivered the following words at the National Conference on Religion and Race in Chicago on January 14, 1963: "History has made us all neighbors. The age of moral mediocrity and complacency has run out. This is a time for radical commitment, for radical action."[12] There he met Dr. Martin Luther King. The two became friends and marched together in Selma two years later. (Steve Zeitlin)

Abraham Joshua Heschel Goes to Selma

BY STEVE ZEITLIN, QUOTING ABRAHAM JOSHUA HESCHEL[11]

With his spiritual audacity undaunted,
Rabbi Heschel marched shoulder to shoulder
with Dr. Martin Luther King
from Selma to Montgomery on Bloody Sunday, 1965,

carrying the scars of the Holocaust
into the battle against racism,
knowing that Jews and Blacks were partners
in one another's liberation.

*It was easier for the children of Israel to cross the Red Sea
than for a Negro to cross certain university campuses*, he said.
Or the Edmund Pettus Bridge.

In a free society, he said, *some are guilty, but all are responsible.*

Marching in the footsteps
of the prophets—
Hosea! Isaiah! Jeremiah!—
Heschel and King set foot on the Edmund Pettus Bridge
into the guns and clubs of the segregated South.

*I felt a sense of the Holy in what I was doing . . .
as though my legs were praying*, he said,

as his feet were marching
on the righteous side of history,
White and Black linked arm in arm,
praying for the world.

JEWels . . . *in Jewish Foods*

Some years ago, my friend Willie Newman, an Israeli sculptor, came up with an idea for bringing peace to the Middle East. City Lore, the organization I direct on the Lower East Side of Manhattan, should host a falafel festival bringing together Israeli and Palestinian cooks along with musical performers. I gave the idea some serious consideration until I saw an article in the *New York Times* a few days later. In "A History of the Middle East in a Humble Chickpea," reporter Jodi Kantor writes, "Many Palestinians believe that Israelis have stolen falafel, a traditional Arab food, and passed it off as what postcards at tourist kiosks all over Israel call 'Israel's National Snack.' . . . Some do more than roll eyeballs. Aziz Shihab, a Palestinian-American and the author of the cookbook 'A Taste of Palestine,' once picked an argument with the owners of an Israeli restaurant in Dallas that served falafel. 'This is my mother's food,' he said. 'This is my grandfather's food. What do you mean you're serving it as your food?'"[1]

The controversy over falafel makes sense. Shaped by Jewish dietary laws (kashrut) as well as by the many places Jews have lived, Jewish cuisine is served in countless variations. Take falafel: there are Persian, Italian, and Egyptian versions, among many others. Falafel originated in Egypt, where it is made from broad beans instead of chickpeas, supposedly "result[ing] in a lighter, fluffier take on the popular snack."[2]

Ashkenazic and Sephardic Jewish cuisines evolved in different ways. For the Ashkenazim in Eastern Europe, potatoes were a perfect food, since the tubers could be stored in cellars through the cold winters. Gefilte ("stuffed" in Yiddish) fish was another. By mixing the selected fish (usually pike or carp) with other ingredients and serving it cold, Jews could make it last throughout the Sabbath, when cooking (or any kind of work) was strictly prohibited. By contrast, the Sephardim in the warm countries of Morocco, Spain, and Greece came to embrace the spicy foods of the locals, salads and fruits, and rice and chickpeas rather than root vegetables.

So for the Shabbat table, Ashkenazic Jews tend to prepare gefilte fish, while Sephardic Jews might make "Moroccan fish" cooked in a spicy tomato sauce. For Hanukkah, when the tradition is to fry something in oil (because of the miracle of finding in the restored Temple a small vessel of olive oil that lasted for eight days rather than one), the Ashkenazim make potato latkes (as children's book writer Roni Schotter puts it, "For Hanukkah there's nothing greater than a grated potato!"), while the Sephardim make *sufganiyot* (jelly doughnuts) or other fried dough. On Passover, the Ashkenazic *haroset* is traditionally made from chopped apples, nuts, cinnamon, and sweet red wine, while the Sephardic version has figs, dates, or raisins, resulting in a thicker paste; in Morocco, this paste is sometimes rolled into balls presented on the seder plate.

Perhaps the most divisive food issue between Ashkenazic and Sephardic Jews has been whether it's okay to eat beans and rice for Passover—Ashkenazis: "No, it's not tradition"; Sephardim: "Yes, they are neither leavened nor unkosher." In 2015 the Rabbinical Assembly (American Conservative rabbinic body) issued a ruling that it was acceptable to add rice and beans to the Passover table, essentially making it okay for Ashkenazic Jews to eat these foods at Passover for the first time in eight centuries.[3]

For Jews of all stripes, eating is serious business. "The less faith a Jew has in the Bible," postulates Michael Wex, "the more Jewish meaning pastrami acquires."[4]

This chapter gathers a multiplicity of Jewish food traditions and stories—my endeavor to "braid the challah."

The Bagel

BY DAVID IGNATOW[5]

I stopped to pick up the bagel
rolling away in the wind,
annoyed with myself
for having dropped it
as if it were a portent.
Faster and faster it rolled,
with me running after it
bent low, gritting my teeth,
and I found myself doubled over
and rolling down the street
head over heels, one complete somersault
after another like a bagel
and strangely happy with myself.

COMMENTARY: To each his own, but I'm with actor Mel Brooks, who plays a two-thousand-year-old man interviewed by comedian Carl Reiner in a midcentury sketch-comedy routine. When asked by Carl what kind of wisdom he can impart from his long life, Mel replies, "Never, ever, run for a bus. There'll always be another." I'm sure he would feel the same way about bagels. (Bob Mankoff)

COMMENTARY: The old-world Shabbat tradition was to bring home a fresh fish—usually a carp, whitefish, or pike, and preferably alive—from the market and put it in a bathtub filled with water. When the *balabusta* (amazing homemaker) was ready, the fish was "fished" out of the bathtub, done in, and prepared—ground up with onion, eggs, matzah meal, and other ingredients, such as carrots and dill, then shaped into oval balls and cooked in simmering water. At the table, the gefilte fish would then be served with a heaping dollop of spicy horseradish. Delicious! (Peninnah Schram)

Storyteller Shirley Kresh Hecker tells a story about a fish named Ike the Pike. Two weeks before Passover, her father brought home a carp and put it in a washtub. In time he became convinced that the carp looked like his friend Levine: "the eyebrows, the one larger eye that held his monocle, the thin lips with the cigar always in place and the high cheekbones." Long story short, her father refused to kill the fish, so her mother ended up killing it. When she finally brought it to the table and uncovered the pot, everyone stared at the sight. Shirley and her siblings had decorated the fish with a face: "a carrot for a nose and raisins for the eyes, and on one eye was my Charlie McCarthy doll's monocle just like the one Mr. Levine wore. In its horseradish mouth was a small piece of celery in place of the cigar. The fish was never eaten."[7] (Steve Zeitlin)

The Fish

BY LILA ZEIGER[6]

I had about as much chance, Mother,
as the carp who thrashed
in your bathtub on Friday,
swimming helplessly back and forth
in the small, hard pool you made
for me,
unaware of how soon you would
pull me from my element,
sever my head just below the gills,
scrape away the iridescence,
chop me into bits and pieces, and
reshape me with your strong hands
to simmer in your special broth.
You bustled about the house,
confident in your design,
while I waited at the edge,
imploring you with glossy eyes
to keep me and love me
just as I was.

Happiness

LINED OUT FROM A RECOLLECTION BY MOISHE SACKS, NEIGHBORHOOD
BAKER AND UNOFFICIAL RABBI OF THE INTERVALE JEWISH CENTER,
THE LAST REMAINING SYNAGOGUE IN THE SOUTH BRONX[8]

I love to braid a challah.
I love to bake a cake.
When I first learned, my hands flew into the process.
I had a weekly schedule:
Monday, a cake called *apple ness*.
Tuesday, strudel.
Wednesday, babkas.
Thursday, this or that.
But at the end of Sunday evening, I was happy,
because by Monday
it went back to *apple ness*.

COMMENTARY: Moishe must have known that *ness* is the Hebrew word for "miracle." (Zev Shanken)

A Jewish Blessing Sung When Placing the Bread in the Oven

ANONYMOUS[9]

Lord of all the world, in your hand is all the blessing.

I come now to revere your holiness and I pray you to bestow your
blessing on the banded goods.

Send an angel to guard the baking, so that all will be well baked, will
rise nicely and not burn,

to honor the holy Sabbath and over which one recites the holy
blessing—

as you blessed the dough of Sarah and Rebecca and our mothers.

My Lord God, listen to my voice;

you are the God who hears the voices of those who

call upon you wholeheartedly. May you be blessed to eternity.

COMMENTARY: As folklorist Hanna Griff-Sleven writes, "This poem is one of many *tekhines*, Jewish women's prayers, in Yiddish, created from the sixteenth through the early twentieth centuries in Eastern and Central Europe and the United States. At the time, women were not taught Hebrew and Aramaic, the languages of Jewish prayer. Also, they were (and still are) not commanded to pray. Rather, their mitzvot (commandments) in the domestic sphere included lighting candles for Shabbat, making challah (bread for the Sabbath), and observing *taharat ha-mishpacha* (family purity laws concerning when a husband and wife are allowed to engage in physical contact). While their husbands had a spiritual outlet through daily synagogue prayer, many of these women also needed to talk to someone about their life experiences: witnessing pogroms, disease, and the daily toil in the home; fear of miscarriages and births; and cooking, baking, and feeding the family. So, quite naturally, they talked to God, in a very personal way. They prayed, created, and wrote their own prayers in Yiddish, the vernacular language of Eastern European Jews. *Tekhines* would be said at the kitchen sink or table—or, in this case, probably in front of the oven."[10] (Steve Zeitlin)

The Atheist

BY STEVE ZEITLIN

Biting into a luscious
Guss'
pickle,
the atheist doubts his faith.

COMMENTARY: In the 1930s, New York City's Lower East Side was a prime place for pushcart peddlers to hawk Jewish and Italian street foods to hungry shoppers. Among the vendors was Isidor "Izzy" Guss, a Russian immigrant who opened his pickle shop, Guss' Pickles, in 1920. The Lower East Side Tenement Museum claims there were about eighty pickle vendors at the time. It's not known whether Guss' pickles were the best or if he simply outlasted them all. But when he died, in 1975, the Lower East Side pickle wars began. According to the Bowery Boys New York City History podcast and website, when Gus died, his shop was sold to the Baker family. In 2004, the Baker family, in turn, sold the business to Patricia Fairhurst, who ran the location on Orchard Street. However, another individual, Andrew Liebowitz of United Pickles, claims that he bought the trademark for Guss' pickles from the Bakers, who agree with his claim that the Fairhursts bought only a lease, not a trademark. So there are, according to the Bowery Boys, "two strains of Guss' pickles in the universe. Leibowitz allegedly has hold of the name, but Fairhurst lays claim to the original recipe."[11] In 2007, Whole Foods began selling Leibowitz's strain of the pickles, but many, including Fairhurst, claim they are simply not true Guss' pickles.

Guss' Pickles left the Lower East Side in 2009. Today, the more recent Pickle Guys shop holds down the fort in what was known as "pickle alley" on Grand Street, a few blocks from Guss's original shop on Hester Street. (Steve Zeitlin)

The Jews and Chinese Food

TRADITIONAL JOKE

If Jewish civilization is five thousand years old
and Chinese civilization is two thousand years old,
what did Jews eat for the first three thousand years?

The Jewish Waiter

TRADITIONAL JOKE

A Jewish waiter at the classic Jewish deli
approaches a table with four Jewish men.
Okay, who ordered the clean glass?

Approaches a table with four Jewish women.
Ladies, is anything okay?

Approaches Abie, an old man, his regular customer, sitting alone.

Taste my soup, says Abie.

What? he says.

I want you should taste my soup.

Why? It's the same soup you've been eating every day for six months!

Taste the soup.

Okay, I'll taste the soup.
Hey, there's no spoon!

Aha!

The Strudel

TRADITIONAL JOKE

The sweet aroma of his daughter's apple strudel
wafts up through the stairway to a dying man's room.

Mmmmmmm. He tries to smile, asks his granddaughter,

*Could you run downstairs
and bring me up my favorite—
a slice of your mama's delicious apple strudel?*

The granddaughter runs downstairs and then back up.

*Sorry, Grandpa.
Ma says it's only for after the funeral.*

Aging Parents

BY MARC WALLACE

In our dating years, Gini and I were visiting my parents' apartment in Philly
when I opened the fridge, found orange juice, and had the urge
to make myself a screwdriver.
Mom, I said, *do you have any*
vodka?
To which she quizzically replied,
latkes?
Laughing, almost at myself, as I realized how poor Mom's hearing had become,
I turned to my father.
Dad, do you have any
vodka?
To which he replied,
matzo?

Now, as my mishearing follows my family's trajectory,
Gini and I laugh and say:

Matzo, latke, vodka?

The Schtup

ADAPTED BY STEVE ZEITLIN FROM A TALE BY STORYTELLER LISA LIPKIN

At Sammy's Roumanian Restaurant,
pouring schmaltz onto our steaks,
my friend and I found ourselves in discussion about the *schtup*.

The "schtup" is a thoroughly Jewish concept, he said,
made possible by a guilt-free relationship with sex.
It's not a fuck, nor is it making love. It's something in between, to be
  enjoyed like a great meal.

Marriage, children, romantic love, praying, even business investments—
  these are the places where Jews find meaning, I replied. *Not in the schtup.*

That's because the schtup is not of the spiritual realm, he said.
It's not anti-heaven, it doesn't belong to hell, but it's part of the earthiness
  that runs
through Jewish culture and folklore—our willingness to accept the body
as part of a duality between the spiritual and the carnal.

Done any schtupping lately? I asked as dessert was being served.

But before he could answer, I got distracted by the cheese blintz

covered in flecks of powdered sugar.
I handed him a fork, and, like participating in a good schtup,
an activity to be savored like a fine wine or a great dessert,
together we indulged.

COMMENTARY: I once asked a rabbi with whom I was having a passionate tryst, "Which do you like more: our conversations or the sex?" He looked perplexed and said, "What's the difference?" That was the perfect response, the one most women dream of: sex and a meeting of the minds had become one.

Still, most of the Jewish men I knew in those days were completely devoid of guilt and thus eschewed emotional responsibility for or meaning in sexual relations. Casual sex is fun, I told myself too. Only later did I realize there was nothing fun about it. The *schtup* became uninteresting to me and fueled my feminist awakening. (Lisa Lipkin)

Fresh Fish Sold Here

TRADITIONAL JOKE RETOLD BY CHERIE KARO SCHWARTZ[12]

Outside of a shop, an immigrant Jewish shopkeeper proudly puts up his sign:

FRESH FISH SOLD HERE.

His know-it-all friend comes along and says, *For a sign, shorter is better. Why have the word* HERE? *Where else would you be selling the fish?*

The shopkeeper blacks out the word "HERE."

FRESH FISH SOLD

And why would you need the word SOLD? *Would you just give the fish away?*
The shopkeeper blacks out "SOLD."

FRESH FISH

Why the word FRESH? *Of course the fish is fresh; would you be selling spoiled fish?*
The shopkeeper blacks out the word "FRESH."

FISH

The shopkeeper is pleased, but not his friend.
And why would you need the word "FISH?" *You can smell them two blocks away!*

How to Make Blintzes

TRADITIONAL JOKE RETOLD BY CHERIE KARO SCHWARTZ

Abe is not a rich man, but he has always dreamed of blintzes.
Sadie, he says, *can you make me some blintzes for Hannukah?*
It's always been my wish.

Blintzes, she says, *are only for those with endless riches.*

If the rich can have blintzes, we poor should have blintzes as well.

Sadie gathers the ingredients.
Well, I have flour. That's a start.
I don't have sugar, but I have honey.
I don't have salt, but I have pepper.
I don't have jam, but I have some juice.
And I only have one egg, not three.
And we are almost out of oil.
And I don't have any butter at all.
But I have the dishes.

She mixes it all up, puts it scoop by scoop
into the big pot, since she doesn't have a pan.
Then she proudly places the blintzes in front of Abe
on a plain wooden dish.

He proudly tastes them.
You know, he says, *I don't know what the big deal is about blintzes.*

2nd Avenue Kosher

BY POET AND INVESTIGATIVE REPORTER DENNIS J. BERNSTEIN,
DESIGNER WARREN LEHRER[13]

at B&H dairy,
    pablo pounds the dough for a wall of challah loaves

        puerto ricano, kosher, yeah!
        bagels with a latin backbeat—
        moses down from spanish harlem

    no such thing!

says simon
in town from tel aviv,

        oh yeah

says pablo,

        one order of cheese blintzes coming up
        and a bowl of cold borscht:

    parve flashes neon from the last century—
but in two thousand ten, spring,
        bernie weinstein cooks
        a mexican plate and serves

        and pablo from across a hundred and tenth
        shapes one challah dough
            after

another
davening in broken english
shaping matzah balls
for the next kosher bowl of soup.

From "The Whole Soul"

BY FORMER U.S. POET LAUREATE PHILIP LEVINE[14]

Is it long as a noodle
or fat as an egg? Is it
lumpy like a potato or
ringed like an oak or an
onion and like the onion
the same as you go toward
the core?

COMMENTARY: Raised in industrial Detroit, Philip Levine was the child of Jewish immigrant parents. His work chronicles the lives of working-class Americans as well as his Jewish inheritance. I love his comparison of the soul to an onion, for the soul is indeed hidden under concentric layers of our spirits, akin to the rings of an onion. Peeling away the layers makes us cry, as we also get closer to what is perhaps the invisible teardrop of our souls. (Steve Zeitlin)

jewels . . . *in Conversations with God*

"THE PEOPLE'S HISTORY IS A HISTORY OF ENCOUNTERS WITH GOD," wrote the twentieth-century rabbi and theologian Leo Baeck. "Every [person] is a question addressed to God."[1]

"Human beings are 'the language of God,'" the eighteenth-century Hasidic leader Menachem-Mendel of Vitebsk once said.[2]

In Jewish tradition, God is imagined and interpreted in endless ways.

"God is not a being outside us, over against us, who manipulates and controls us and raises some people over others," feminist theologian Judith Plaskow writes. "God is the source and wellspring of life in its infinite diversity. God—as our foremothers seem to have known—is present in all aspects of life, but present not just as father and protector but as one who empowers us to act creatively ourselves."[3]

Rabbi Abraham Joshua Heschel notes that he never asked God for fame, wisdom, or power. "I asked for wonder instead of happiness, and You gave them to me."[4]

Neither truth, belief, dogma, nor obedience captures the core relationship of Jews to God, the philosopher Walter Kaufman says. "There is another word that really goes to the heart of the matter: intimacy."[5]

A midrash suggests God's perspective: "When you are my witnesses, I am God—when you are not my witnesses, I am, as it were, not God."[6]

And then there's the common contradiction "I don't know if I believe in religion, but I certainly don't want to let God down."

The poems that follow paint a picture of Jews as questioners. Wistfully, they speculate that "there is a God"; "there isn't a God"; "there may be a God"; "there can't be a God"; "you should pray to God"; "you shouldn't bother to pray"; "you may as well pray." God may be the ruler of the universe, a passerby, a model of goodness, a goad toward justice, the greatest metaphor, or, as one Jewish comedian put it, "a serious underachiever."

The Messiah #1

LINED OUT FROM MICHAEL GOLD'S *JEWS WITHOUT MONEY*[7]

Old Barney was one of the characters on our street.
Wore a cloak green with age and stuffed with rags.
We watched Barney as he sat silent on the stoop,
pilgrim's staff in hand.

Only one question made Barney talk.

What are you waiting for?

I am waiting for the Messiah, my children.

And what will the Messiah bring you, Barney?

A glass of cream soda.

I believed the Messiah was coming too.
It was the one point in the Jewish religion I could understand.
We had no Santa Claus, but we had a Messiah.

COMMENTARY: In another story, a Chelm local asks the rabbi, "Which is more important, the sun or the moon?" The rabbi retorts, "What a silly question! The moon, of course! It shines at night when we truly need it. But who needs the sun to shine when it is already broad daylight?" (Peninnah Schram)

The Messiah #2

TRADITIONAL JOKE

In Chelm, the town of fools,
the elders worried that a sudden appearance by the Messiah
would find the village unprepared.

So they offered Shmuel
one ruble a year
to perch on a cliff high above Chelm
as a harbinger for the Messiah.

Thrilled, Shmuel
ran home to tell his brother,
a *macher*—a big shot—at the temple.

No, no, no, his brother said.
Awaiting the Messiah—
that's a crucial task.
You must go back to them,
demand five rubles, ten rubles a year.

Shmuel said,
One ruble a year is not a lot of money, Brother.
But awaiting the Messiah?
That's a very steady job.

COMMENTARY: The *Tikkun Hazzot* (the ritual of Jews reciting prayers at midnight to mourn the Temple's destruction) is thought to have been rooted in a prayer intended to hasten the Messiah.

Jewish tradition includes a number of stories about hastening the Messianic Age. The fifteenth-century kabbalist Joseph della Reyna believed that the Jews needed to release the Messiah from the forces of evil, to loosen the chains that had kept him from freeing the people of Israel. According to one story, Della Reyna and his followers uttered holy names and instigated what became a losing battle with the angels, who proceeded to kill the followers and transform Della Reyna into a black dog. To other kabbalists, this proved that the Messiah must not be brought down to earth prematurely. A few centuries later, Rabbi Nachman of Breslov perhaps more sensibly said that the Messiah will not descend until people stop waiting for his arrival, are truly pious, and are not expecting a reward.[9] (Steve Zeitlin)

This poem brings to mind French author Guy de Maupassant's short story "The Venus of Braniza." In this story, a greatly respected talmudist is married to a very beautiful wife who is known as "the Venus of Braniza." One day the Venus of Braniza asks her husband, "When will the Messiah come?" He responds: "The Messiah will come when either all the Jews become good or all the Jews become evil." When he goes out of town to resolve a Jewish dilemma, his wife begins an affair with the captain of the Hussars. When the talmudist returns earlier than expected, he sees his wife—and evidence that another man has been with her—and exclaims: "Woman! Are you out of your mind?" She replies: "I am in full possession of my senses." With a knowing smile hovering around her voluptuous lips, she continues, "But since all the Jews will never become good, must I not also do my evil part to attract the Messiah so he may come and redeem us poor Jews?" (Peninnah Schram)

Closer

BY AARON ZEITLIN, TRANSLATED FROM THE
YIDDISH BY MORRIS M. FAIERSTEIN[8]

The wall clock strikes twelve.
The darkness moans, the darkness groans:
Closer by a day to death,
closer to death.

Grandfather gets up for *tikkun hazot*.
The candle in his hand says:
Closer by a day the coming of the Messiah,
closer by a day.

Wrestling with God

BY CARTOONIST AND FORMER CARTOON EDITOR
OF THE *NEW YORKER* BOB MANKOFF

All night long
Jacob wrestled with the Archangel
on the Jabbok River shores—
till the sun rose.

Then Jacob realized
the Archangel was God—
not outside the fray but part of it—

and that he was not only losing the match
but witnessing the defeat of the human soul at the hands of God.

So he said to the Archangel,
This time
you bested me—
how about two out of three?

COMMENTARY: The smart money is still on God. As the writer
Damon Runyon once said, "The race is not always to the swift
nor the battle to the strong, but don't bet against them." (Bob
Mankoff)

Somebody Up There Likes Me

TRADITIONAL JOKE RETOLD BY BOB MANKOFF

A man is looking over a cliff
when he slips—
and just as he's falling
catches hold of a branch,
looks up to the heavens,
and cries,
> *Is there anybody up there who can help me?!*

The Lord says,
> *I will help you.*
> *Just let go of the branch*
> *and you will float earthward slowly like a feather*
> *and gently, gently wend your way to the ground unharmed.*

The man glances upward again.
> *Is there anybody else up there who can help me?*

It's All Relative

TRADITIONAL JOKE RETOLD BY PENINNAH SCHRAM

A man queries God,
God, tell me, what is a million years like to you?

God thinks and replies slowly,
A million years is like a minute.

Then the man asks,
God, tell me, what is a million dollars like to you?

God smiles and answers quickly,
A million dollars? A million dollars to me is like a penny.

Finally the man asks,
God, would you loan me a penny?

God laughs and pauses four beats. . . .
Wait a minute.

COMMENTARY: One day I read a couplet in a psalm that struck me as strange. Psalm 90, verse 4, says: "For a thousand years in Your sight / Are but as yesterday when it is past." Wow, I thought—and then it triggered this joke, which I might have heard a thousand—or was it a million?—years ago. (Peninnah Schram)

Tevye the Milkman Said

LINED OUT FROM THE STORY "TEVYE STRIKES IT RICH"
BY YIDDISH WRITER SHOLEM ALEICHEM[10]

Oh, my dear Lord.
You're a long-suffering God, a good God, a great God,
they say. *You're merciful and fair.*
Perhaps you can explain to me, then,
why is it that some folks have everything and others have nothing
     twice over?

But it's just that you're a Jew in this world. A Jew must have confidence
     and faith.
He must believe, first, that there is a God, and, second, that if there is,
and that if it's all the same to Him, and if it isn't too much trouble,
He can make things a little better for the likes of you.

COMMENTARY: The beloved short stories of Sholem Aleichem (1859–1916) became the basis for the hit musical *Fiddler on the Roof*, in which Tevye the Milkman poses similar questions. In his essay "Tevye's Query," Rabbi Dr. Yaakov Brawer quotes the beloved *Fiddler* lyrics "Would it spoil some vast eternal plan / if I were a wealthy man?" and reflects: "Tevye is no theologian. [Yet] Tevye has raised one of the most enigmatic and recondite issues in religious thought. . . . The impecunious milkman would undoubtedly be shocked to learn that the answer to his question is: yes, it would spoil some vast eternal plan if he were a wealthy man. . . . The Talmud (Taanit 25a) relates that Rabbi Elazar ben Pedat, who was exceedingly poor, once fell ill and required bleeding, a common medical treatment in ancient times. Following the procedure, he wished to strengthen himself by taking nourishment, but he was so poor that all he had was a garlic peel. He ate the garlic peel and fell into a faint, during which he had a vision of the Divine Presence (*Shechinah*). He inquired of the *Shechinah* how long he was to be subjected to such grinding poverty, and was answered: 'Elazar, my son, do you wish that I destroy the universe and reconstruct it, so that you can perhaps be created in a time favorable to prosperity?'"[11] (Steve Zeitlin)

My Aunt's Ninetieth Birthday

ADAPTED BY STEVE ZEITLIN FROM A QUIP BY JEWISH CULTURAL ACTIVIST
ANN KATZ DURING ONE OF ZEITLIN'S TALKS ON JEWISH HUMOR

My aunt was celebrating her ninetieth birthday and her family threw her
    a lovely party.
Her oldest son said, *Mama, I think you should get up now*
and say something to your guests.

And, I swear to God, she got up and said,
I am very, very lucky.
God has been very, very good to me.
He should only live and be well.

The Tailor's Prayer

TRADITIONAL TALE

Dear God,

You want me to repent for my sins,
but my sins have been so small.

There were times I failed to return
a piece of leftover cloth to my customers.
I even ate food that was not kosher.

Now take Yourself, God.
You have robbed mothers of their babes,
sent multitudes to untimely deaths,
millions to the gas chambers,
caused poverty, hunger, disease.

Though Your travesties are huge
and mine are only small,

and while it's true that I am only me
and You are You,
let us plan a fair exchange.

I'll forgive You, and You forgive me.

COMMENTARY: In other variations of this Hasidic story, someone like the Baal Shem Tov or Rabbi Levi Yitzhak of Berditchev offers God the exchange of forgiveness, but most often it's a poor man, either Berel the tailor or Moshe the innkeeper, who strikes the bargain with God: "You forgive me, and I'll forgive You." In some ways, these ordinary men have similarities with Bonshe Schweig, author I. L. Peretz's meek protagonist who suffers through life's indignities only to blow his one chance to make a major deal before letting God off the hook.

Yet haven't we all found ourselves "bargaining" with God by asking for something we lack and offering to do something in return? (Peninnah Schram).

A Pair of Pants

TRADITIONAL TALE[12]

A man brings a pair of pants to a tailor for repair.
The tailor tells him to come back in a few days.

He comes back in three days.
The pants, says the tailor, *are not ready.*

Frustrated, the man comes back six days later.
The pants are not ready.

He comes back ten days later.
The pants are ready.

Furious, the man rants,
Why did you take so long?
For heaven's sake, God created the world in six days!

Ah, said the tailor, *but look at this world.*
Then look at this beautiful pair of pants.

The Do-Over

BY STEVE ZEITLIN, INSPIRED BY A CONVERSATION WITH
WRITER AND HISTORIAN RICHARD RABINOWITZ

When we were kids in Brooklyn,
children of religious Jewish immigrants
playing on the streets,
God never entered our lives

except for in a "do-over"—
when the super or your mother
yelled out the window
or a car drove by
just before the broomstick bat struck the pink Spaldeen—
the play disrupted.

Back in the day when first base was a lamppost,
second base a manhole cover,
third base your little brother,

someone would yell, *Hindu, do it again!*
(nobody knew where that crazy phrase came from),
and the play would be repeated,
and God would come down
and intercede in human affairs to ensure
the play turned out just as it would have
had it not been interrupted.

The DNA in My Coffee—A True Story

ADAPTED BY STEVE ZEITLIN FROM THE STORY "GOD
AND DNA OVER COFFEE" BY LISA LIPKIN[13]

Once again, my father and I squabbled about God over breakfast.
I just don't understand how I could have come from you! I said.

DNA, he replied, as only a scientist could.

Can't God exist without the lab reports to back it up?

It depends on what you mean by God, he said.
To me, God is the sum total of all the intelligence in the universe.
To others, it's something else, something more emotional, perhaps.
Pass the danishes, please.

Can't you ever just take a leap of faith? I asked.

Faith, kiddo, is anything where the evidence is missing.

Then why be Jewish, Dad?

It's about belonging to a group. Humanity's family.

What about the Torah?

Moses went up there and scribbled it out.
It's a nice set of moral laws.
Get me my coat from the closet, will you?

But, Dad, you married a Holocaust survivor,
and your mother's youth, her entire family, was stolen from her by the
   pogroms in Russia.
Does this mean nothing to you?

Kiddo, it means that somehow humankind still has potential for goodness.
After all, the fact that you're here is proof of that.

Just then my phone rang.

I ran for the receiver and, from the kitchen, I could see him preparing to
  leave.

He buttoned his coat collar, pulled a wool cap over his ears,

and kissed the mezuzah as he walked out the door.

Deconstructing Heaven

ADAPTED BY STEVE ZEITLIN FROM A TALE
RETOLD BY RABBI AVRAHAM WEISS[14]

It is said that when Rebbe Moshe Leib of Sassof passed away,
angels set out to guide him on the journey to heaven,

but the only way to get to heaven is to pass through hell.

When the Rebbe saw the broken souls of hell,
he refused to advance
until all those who suffered
could join him in heaven.

He raised hell
until a heavenly court
ruled that for every good deed of Moshe Leib,
he could bring one and only one soul to heaven.

All ended well:
Moshe Leib had done as many good deeds
as there were souls in hell.

So what does this story tell us of heaven and of hell?
Rav Carlson: each of your good deeds shall free a soul from hell.
Rabbi Weiss: human beings are partners in the process of redemption.

Levi Yitzhak Burns the Evidence

TRADITIONAL TALE

Once, there was a heavenly courtroom, empty
except for a table, and on it stood
the scales of justice. On one side was a box,
heavy with the records of humankind's evil deeds
that year;
and on the other side, a small case
holding the files of the year's good deeds.
A sigh filled the universe
as the scale tipped toward evil.

Suddenly,
Rabbi Levi Yitzhak of Berditchev,
defender of the Jews, left his place
in Paradise, barged into the courtroom,
reached into the box of evil deeds,
pulled out a sheaf,
and threw it into
the fires of hell.
The scale was balanced at last.

Then—Lord help him—Levi Yitzhak
came face to face with Satan,
who, in his desperation to possess
the souls of all humanity, removed
his crown and placed it
on the side of the scale
weighed down with evil deeds.
I have you, Levi Yitzhak! he said.

But then God placed heaven
and earth on the other side
of the scale. *Can't you see?* God said.
The soul of Levi Yitzhak is worth
the universe to me.

Six Lines

BY AARON ZEITLIN, TRANSLATED FROM THE YIDDISH BY ROBERT FRIEND

I know that in this world no one needs me,
me, a word-beggar in the Jewish graveyard.
Who needs a poem, especially in Yiddish?

Only what is hopeless on this earth has beauty,
and only the ephemeral is godly
and humility is the only true rebellion.

COMMENTARY: I'm reminded of a lovely quote by Czech statesman and writer Vaclav Havel: "A human action becomes genuinely important when it springs from the soil of a clear-sighted awareness of the temporality and the ephemerality of everything human. It is only this awareness that can breathe any greatness into an action."[15] In actions such as lighting or extinguishing candles on the Sabbath, Jewish tradition honors the ephemeral. (Steve Zeitlin)

To the Rescue

TRADITIONAL JOKE

A Jew is stranded at sea, bobbing on the ocean waves.

A man in a rowboat spots him from a distance,
rows toward him with all his might,
shouts and reaches out . . .

Do not worry, cries the Jew. *God will help me.*

A woman on a cruise ship sees him. A passenger lowers an inner tube
   on a rope.

Do not worry, cries the Jew. *God will help me.*

As the cruise ship sails away, the captain sees a helicopter approaching,
descending, and hovering just above the flailing man.

Do not worry, cries the Jew. *God will help me.*

The helicopter flies on.

The Jew drowns.

When he gets to heaven, he implores God,

Why didn't you help me?

Help you? I sent a rowboat, a cruise ship, and a helicopter.

Lifeline

TRADITIONAL TALE[16]

A Jew suffering the slings and arrows of misfortune turns his head toward God.

Lord, he says, *this world is plagued with anguish, hopelessness, malevolence, depression, and despair. Why do you not send help?*

My friend, I did send help.
I sent you.

10 JEWels . . . *on the Meaning of Life*

FOR EACH OF US, THE SEARCH FOR MEANING IS THE ULTIMATE pilgrimage. How do Jews in particular understand this search?

The day after I raised this question with Peninnah Schram, she found herself in a stark white doctor's waiting room with one other patient, an Orthodox Jew. So she said to him, out of the blue: "I have a question for you: From a Jewish perspective, what is the meaning of life?" He answered seriously, "To live a spiritual life. To be an ethical person. To acknowledge God."

Later, Peninnah told me she believes that a good Jewish life is also a partnership with God. The Sea of Reeds did not part when Moses waved a wand, she said, but when Nachshon ben Aminadav, head of the tribe of Judah, jumped into the sea. "The miracle was brought on," Peninnah explained, "when someone had enough faith to do something."

Peninnah ended our conversation with a joke: "Moishe goes to heaven and asks God, 'Why didn't you ever help me win the lottery?' God responds, 'Did you ever think to buy a ticket?'" I understand this to mean that we humans need to be active players in the partnership with God. Rabbi Tarfon suggested that we need not finish the work that God began, but neither are we at liberty to desist from it.[1] We need to be creative in whatever ways we choose to move the human enterprise forward. We don't simply want to be spectators at the pageant.

Marc Kaminsky emphasizes the ethical imperative "to shelter the widow, the orphan, and the stranger" (Exod. 22:21–24), something many Jews understand collectively, given that, historically, they were often strangers in a strange land themselves.

In these and other ways, Jews speak of *tikkun olam*: the repairing of a tear in the fabric of creation to make the world whole again. We need to endeavor, as Rabbi Abraham Joshua Heschel writes, to "sew the threads of temporality into the fabric of eternity."[2] We need to become the tailor and the seamstress.

The underpinning for this idea is the Jewish call to choose life. In a Yom Kippur sermon, Rabbi Edward Schecter—who almost died from a rare ailment as a boy, lost two wives to illness, and survived cancer—told his congregation that, according to Jewish tradition, if a wedding procession encounters a funeral procession at a crossroads, the wedding procession must go first, because Jews are commanded to choose life (as Schecter did). Before his death, Moses passed on this charge from God to the people of Israel: "See, I set before you this day life and good, death and evil . . . I have put before you life and death, blessing and curse. Choose life—so that you and your children after you will live" (Deut. 30:15, 19).

That is why, Rabbi Schecter explained, the German rabbi and theologian Leo Baeck ignored the advice of passive resistance activist Mahatma Gandhi, who in the years leading up to the Holocaust suggested that the Jews commit suicide en masse to shock the conscience of the world. Baeck responded: "We Jews know that the commandment of God is to live."[3]

Ultimately, as the following tales and jokes attest, our task is to imbue life with meaning. Folklorist Daniel Sheehy suggests, "The meaning of life is the meaning you give it."[4] As theologian Elliot Ginsburg writes: "On this earth, we each create *olam u-melo'o*, Hebrew for 'a world replete with meanings.'"[5] Life means enormously.

The Meaning of Meaning

BY BOB HOLMAN

And so the philosophical, philological, semiotical, deconstructivist,
mostly Jewish poets
argued late into the night.

What's the meaning of meaning?
What's the purpose of purpose?

Oh, I get it, one said. *The answer's not related to the question,*
and nothing's on purpose,
the purpose of which is to assure you
that's there's no meaning to meaning in the first place.

But in the second place . . .

COMMENTARY: This poem reminds me of columnist Thomas Friedman's June 14, 2017, *New York Times* op-ed, "Solving the Korea Crisis by Teaching a Horse to Sing."[6] Friedman was sitting in a hotel restaurant in Seoul one morning when he heard the news that, as he put it, "North Korea had just fired a short-range ballistic missile that had landed in the sea off its east coast." In response, he said, the United States and the rest of the world decided to do . . . nothing. Friedman then retold this fable of the horse, which applies to so many situations in which doing nothing might prove to be just the right thing. He concluded: "And that is our North Korea policy. Waiting for *something* to solve this insoluble problem. Waiting for a horse to sing." (In different versions of the joke, the horse may learn to fly–or sing. Peninnah Schram)

Who Knows?

ADAPTED BY CARTOONIST AND STORYTELLER FLASH ROSENBERG
FROM ONE OF HER FATHER'S FAVORITE JOKES

Two Jews arguing over the Talmud, and
accidently strolling outside their shtetl,
find themselves
captured,
jailed,
condemned
to immediate death by the czar.

The clever scholar proposes:
Give us a year to live
and we'll teach your horse to fly.

The other scholar panics, mutters in his ear:
Are you crazy?
We can't teach a horse to fly.
We're certain to be put to death.

The clever scholar whispers back:
A year is a long time.
Many things can happen—
the czar might die.
We might die.
Or who knows?
Maybe the horse will fly!

Hineni

BY FLASH ROSENBERG

Went to Hebrew school for eight years. Cannot speak it.
Learned to make the sounds of Hebrew. To recite blessings.
If I ever need a sandwich in Israel, I'll have to pray for one.

Last day of class, found the nerve to ask: *Why did I have to study Hebrew three times a week for eight long years, when all I learned is to hate Hebrew?*
Rabbi Krinsky explained: *All the Hebrew you need was taught the first day.*

What? Shalom? And I was done?

Not shalom, but Hineni—*Hebrew for "Here I am."*

You must be present,
not only to respond to your name during attendance
but to help whenever you are called upon,
however you are needed.

The prayer to give thanks for your talents is to use them.

COMMENTARY: *Hineni* is a luminous word in the Jewish tradition. When God called upon Abraham to sacrifice his son, Abraham answered, "*Hineni.*" When the angel of God later prevented Abraham from performing this horrific act, Abraham once again cried, "*Hineni.*" Generations later, when Moses stood before the burning bush, he, too, responded, "*Hineni.*" Some rabbis suggest that *Hineni* is meant to remind God that God shares responsibility for what befalls human beings, just as the humans standing before God accept their responsibility by invoking *Hineni*, "Here I am."[7] (Steve Zeitlin)

The Angel of Death

ADAPTED BY STEVE ZEITLIN FROM AN ESSENTIALLY TRUE
STORY IN HOWARD SCHWARTZ'S *TREE OF SOULS*[8]

Toward the end of his life, scholar Howard Schwartzbaum,
working on a book about the Angel of Death,
told this story of Rabbi Judah Loew,
a mystic in sixteenth-century Prague during the plague years.

One day, Loew, glancing through a synagogue window,
spied the Angel gripping a sharpened knife and a long list of names.
Sneaking up behind the dreaded Angel,
he snatched the list from his hand,
sparing hundreds from the calamity to come.

On a break from his studies, Schwartzbaum
ran into the famed Israeli folklorist Dov Noy,
who asked, *When do you wish to finish your mighty tome?*

I'm taking my time, Schwartzbaum said, *because the Angel of Death
would dare not take me before my book is done.*

The Angel of Death just laughed,
waved a torn sheet in his hand.

Schwartzbaum's dead.
The book remains undone.

The Land

ADAPTED BY STEVE ZEITLIN FROM A TRADITIONAL TALE

The rabbi and the imam
argue peaceably over
the holiest of lands.

This land was promised to our people
from the days of Abraham.

But my people are living on this land.

A child passing by overhears their conversation.
The dilemma is a simple one, he says,
easily overcome.

He puts his ear to the ground.

So what does it tell you, my child?
asks the rabbi.

What do you hear?
asks the imam.

It says,
"This land belongs to none of you.
You belong to the land."[9]

If Not Higher!

ADAPTED BY STEVE ZEITLIN FROM THE SHORT
STORY "IF NOT HIGHER!" BY I. L. PERETZ[10]

When the Rabbi of Nemirov
would disappear before the Days of Awe,
his supplicants believed he was visiting heaven.

One day, a skeptic followed the rabbi,
saw him grab an ax from under his bed,
walk into the woods,
chop down a tree,
saw it to pieces,
tie up the wood,
visit an old, sick widow,
and offer her kindling for her fire.

So, a supplicant asked the skeptic,
did the rabbi visit heaven?

He replied, *If not higher!*

COMMENTARY: The journalist Anne Roiphe writes: "The main pillar of the Jewish religion is remembering. It is the telling and retelling each year of stories from the past. . . . 'Remember this'; 'Remember that.' The past is part of every Jewish child's experience. . . . This makes Jews continually the witnesses of their own past, and gives the odd flavor to their reasonings—as if history were happening in both the vertical and the horizontal time line, as if things moved forward and stayed still at the same time."[12] I am reminded of this wonderful perception of Holocaust survivor and Jewish theologian Viktor E. Frankl in his classic book *Man's Search for Meaning*: "In the past, nothing is irretrievably lost but rather, on the contrary, everything is irrevocably stored and treasured."[13] (Steve Zeitlin)

Time All at Once

ADAPTED BY STEVE ZEITLIN FROM A STORY BY
LAWYER AND ACTIVIST CAROLINE HARRIS[11]

Like my mother's stories
that always go way back to how she met her husband, to her birth,
    or before,
our seders go back to the beginning.

PAST. The haggadah reaches back to the beginning of time, to Creation.
We remember when we first lit and blessed the holiday candles,
separating light and darkness to start the story as it begins in Genesis.
Later, we fled from Egypt with no time for the bread to rise.

PRESENT. The matzah, the unleavened bread that has come to
    symbolize the past,
is hidden and becomes the playful present as young children are
    rewarded
when they find the *afikomen*.

We eat heartily with a dash of bitterness about the brother who won't
    join us,
sadness about the aunt who died.

FUTURE. A story that begins with Creation can only end in the far
    distant future,
beyond time,
after Elijah, in the world to come—in *olam ha-ba*.

Yes, the haggadah concludes "Next year in Jerusalem!"—
a hope for the physical place Jews consider home—
but beyond this lies the existential hope:

someday, in the world to come,
all of us will enter the Land of Milk and Honey,
the perfect world of peace, freedom, and justice.

Soul Sight

ADAPTED BY MARC KAMINSKY AND STEVE ZEITLIN
FROM HOWARD SCHWARTZ'S *TREE OF SOULS*[14]

When losses become too much
to bear, when despair
overwhelms, and you wander
in darkness, alone,

stop where
you are, and call
upon Yode'a, the Angel
of Losses. His lesser

angels are handed shovels
to dig for what's been
lost, but when all
that's lost can't be found

by digging, stop
once more and let Yode'a
reach you in the dark.
Let him teach you to allow

the light inside your soul
to guide your steps.

COMMENTARY: Yode'a is an angel thought to have been created by Rabbi Nachman of Breslov to address the nature of loss in human life. The name evokes the Hebrew word *yada* (one who knows), suggesting that the angel is meant to recall or return all that has been lost.[15] In his essay "The Secret Jewish History of *Star Wars*," cultural critic Seth Rogovoy—speculating, of course—suggests that Yode'a's name might have been the inspiration behind film's director George Lucas's choice to "name . . . the wise old man Yoda, who passed away at the very Biblical age of 900 in 1983's 'Return of the Jedi.'. . . . [The name] . . . translates as 'one who knows' in Hebrew."[16] (Steve Zeitlin)

The Burning Twig

ADAPTED BY STEVE ZEITLIN FROM A TRADITIONAL
TALE RETOLD BY ROBERT J. BERNSTEIN

Temple Beth Shalom
holds a bonfire cookout
on a fall afternoon.

As the congregants gather around the fire,
Jacob announces with great fanfare
that he is abandoning the congregation,
going his own way.

The rabbi remains silent.
He takes a stick from the edge of the bonfire
and sets it to the side, separate from the others.

For a moment it blazes, then quickly burns out.

Jacob decides to stay.

Oy

LINED OUT FROM A SPONTANEOUS OBSERVATION BY
STUDENT OF JEWISH FOLK CULTURE ELI LEVINE

Can mean:
Oy, I'm worried about my son—
I haven't heard from him in weeks.

Oy,
imagine how it must feel to lose a child.

Oy,
isn't this the most beautiful simcha (joyous occasion)?

All this in one tiny word,
the entire history of the Jewish people:
Oy.

COMMENTARY: My friend Penina Adelman tells the backstory to "Oy" in my book *Chosen Tales*. Eli Levine was a student in her class on Jewish folklore at Hebrew College: "But," she says, "he was a student in name only. An elderly gentleman whose whole being came to life as soon as he started speaking, Eli was an expert in Jewish folklore. He had lived it, breathed it, and passed it on both in *di alter haim* (the Old Country) in Volkovisk, Poland, and here in *di goldene medine* (the United States). When Eli was discussing the expressiveness of Hasidic *nigunnim* (melodies without words), how the *nigun* was so versatile that it could convey whatever the mood and intention of the singer happened to be at the time, he said, 'It's the same with the word *oy*,' and spontaneously [said these words]."

Months later, Penina learned that Eli had cancer and didn't have long to live. "*Oy* can mean that too," she said.

Penina promised Eli that she would tell his stories as often as she could. "I think he was able to die with greater ease knowing that his stories would live on," she wrote. "Every time you tell a story of a person who has died, you are keeping alive the memory of their name."[17] (Peninnah Schram)

The Philosopher

TRADITIONAL JOKE[18]

The revered philosopher from Chelm,
the town of fools,
ponders the dichotomy of life and death.
Life is filled with so much tragedy, sadness, calamity, and catastrophe
that death should not be thought a misfortune.

People should consider themselves lucky,
he concludes,
never to have been born.
But how many are so fortunate?

Not one in ten thousand.

Life

TRADITIONAL JOKE[19]

Two elderly women at a Catskill Mountain resort.
The first one says,
Boy, the food in this place is terrible.

The second one says,
I know—and such tiny portions.

Isn't that the way life goes?
So much misery and unhappiness,
yet

it's all over too quickly.

The Razbash on Old Age

BY ZEV SHANKEN

Whoever destroys a soul, it is considered as if he destroyed an entire world. And whoever saves a life, it is considered as if he saved an entire world. (Mishnah Sanhedrin 4:9)

The Razbash asks, "Why does it read 'an entire world'? Why not simply 'world'?"

> When you die,
> everything you learned
> searches for a new learner,
> but everything you did not learn
> ceases to exist for eternity.
>
> That is why it is incumbent
> to learn as much as you can,
> even in old age, until your last breath.
> The *entire* world needs you.

COMMENTARY: I consider this among my favorite poems. I have taken it to heart. Now I encourage myself to read more and watch more documentaries than I used to, and I am less afraid of an adage set forth by Vicksburg, Mississippi, mule trader Ray Lum: "You live and you learn. Then you die and forget it all." Zev's poem gives us a new reason for learning. (Steve Zeitlin)

Doctor, Doctor

ADAPTED BY STEVE ZEITLIN FROM A TRADITIONAL JOKE
RETOLD BY STORYTELLER DORIS KIRSHENBLATT[20]

A man in his late seventies visits his doctor:

What should I do so I can really enjoy my wealth
and live a lot longer?

The doctor enumerated:

Don't smoke, don't drink, don't eat all that fatty food.
No more briskets or corned beef sandwiches.
Eat much less, steam your food, rest, don't risk sex.

When the doctor finished,
the man said:

Doctor, if I do all this, will I live longer?

He said, *I don't know if you'll live longer,*
but it will seem like a very long time.

Yizkor

BY ZEV SHANKEN

What's good about remembering the dead
is I can do with them whatever I want.
So they join me at their best.

They make friends with the other dead in my life,
share insights on my usual mistakes,
and remind me that they see the full picture.

Then they say, *Don't worry about us.*
We got through it just fine.
It's you we want to bless.

It's always worth it.
You're always worth it.
Don't worry. It's going to be great.

COMMENTARY: *Yizkor* is a special memorial prayer for the
departed, recited in the synagogue on four holidays throughout
the year: the last day of Passover, the second day of Shavuot,
Shemini Atzeret, and Yom Kippur. Once, as I paged through a
prayer book during a *Yizkor* service, I began to imagine all the
dead people I knew together, at their best, revived and giving me
advice. When I asked how *they* were doing, they told me things I
put in the poem. (Zev Shanken)

The Razbash on Forgiveness

BY ZEV SHANKEN

If a deathbed confession might scare the patient,
do not make the offer. The Sages explain,
The agony of dying is atonement enough.

If confessing makes dying worse, do not confess.
If confessing makes dying holy, confess.
God grants atonement either way.

What insightful ancient people
invented this clever, gentle God,
who loves us so that even in death
we lose only our life!

You are forgiven.
You are always forgiven.
Dying is atonement enough.

COMMENTARY: Since there was no rabbi in the area when my mother was on her deathbed, I considered reading her the death-bed confession found in some prayer books, but then I read the following cautionary text in *The Complete ArtScroll Siddur* and was dissuaded:

"If a sick person is near death, Heaven forbid, someone should recite the following confession with him. However, it is required that this be done in such a way that his morale not be broken because this may even hasten death. He should be told, 'Many have confessed and did not die and many who did not confess died anyway. In reward for your having confessed, may you live, but everyone who confesses has a share in the World to Come. If the patient cannot speak, he should confess in his heart. One who is unsophisticated should not be asked to confess because it may break his spirit and cause him to weep.'"[21]

I was proud that my religion uses its insights into human nature in such a compassionate way. (Zev Shanken)

The Womb

TRADITIONAL TALE RETOLD BY RABBI EDWARD SCHECTER

A man asks his rabbi, *Is there life*
after death? The rabbi says, *Imagine*

you're a twin awaiting birth. You
say to your brother, "This world is
all there is."

The other contends, "I
believe there is a world to come."

The two of you continue growing
from a fishlike to a human form

over what seems a limitless
expanse of time—

and then you're born.
To both, a grand surprise.

So, says the Rabbi, *who is*
to say what happens when we die?

Moishe's Wisdom

LINED OUT FROM MOISHE SACKS'S COMMENTS IN
THE GRAND GENERATION DOCUMENTARY[22]

I don't think I'll know death.

I know only two things:
the present, how to live.

The present, how to live
does not include death.

The Angel of Forgetfulness

LINED OUT FROM DARA HORN'S NOVEL *THE WORLD TO COME*[23]

Before being born, his mother explained,
babies go to . . . a different kind of school.
The angels teach each baby the entire Torah,
along with all the secrets of the universe.

Then, just before each baby is born,
an angel puts its finger in the cleft right below the baby's nose and
whispers to the child: "Sh—don't tell."
And the baby forgets,

so that for the rest of his life
he will always have to pay attention to the world,
and to everything that happens in it,
to try to remember all the things he's forgotten.

COMMENTARY: In Jewish tradition, babies learn all the "dos"
and "do nots," the "shalls" and "shall nots," before they are born,
but then they come into the world right in the middle of things
and have to determine right and wrong in the context of their
own lives and times. I believe this deeply Jewish idea is rooted
in one of Plato's most famous Socratic dialogues. The other
main speaker, Meno, asks Socrates if he can prove the truth of
his strange claim that "all learning is recollection." In response,
Socrates calls over an enslaved boy and, after establishing that the
boy is not versed in mathematics, asks him to solve a geometry
problem. The way Socrates frames his question makes it appear
that the boy's ability to answer correctly proves that the boy
already had this knowledge within him; Socrates's question just
made it easier for the boy to recollect it. To Socrates, this episode
indicates that the soul is immortal, since the boy must have
known the answer all along. (Rabbi Edward Schecter)

The Laughing Man

LINED OUT FROM ELIE WIESEL'S *SOULS ON FIRE*, BASED ON
WRITINGS ATTRIBUTED TO RABBI NACHMAN OF BRESLOV[24]

Once upon a time there was a country
that encompassed all the countries of the world.
And in that country there was a town
that incorporated all the towns of the country;
and in that town there was a street,
in which were gathered all the streets of the town;
and on that street there was a house
that sheltered all the houses of the street;
and in that house there was a room,
and in that room there was a man,
and that man personified all the men of all countries.
And that man laughed and laughed—
no one had ever laughed like that before.

WIESEL'S RESPONSE

LINED OUT FROM ELIE WIESEL'S *SOULS ON FIRE*[25]

Who is that man? The Creator laughing at his creation?
Man sending Him back his laughter as an echo
or perhaps as a challenge?

The Fiftieth Gate

LINED OUT FROM A PASSAGE BY RABBI BORUCH OF
MEDZHYBIZH, AS RECOUNTED BY MARTIN BUBER[26]

I know what is hidden in your heart, said the rabbi.
You have passed through the fifty gates of reason.
You begin with a question and think up an answer—
and the first gate opens to a new question!
And again you plumb it, find the solution, fling open the second gate—
and look into a new question.

On and on like this, deeper and deeper,
until you have forced open the fiftieth gate.
There you stare at a question whose answer no man has ever found,
for if there were one who knew it,
there would no longer be freedom of choice.
But if you dare to probe still further, you plunge into the abyss.

So I should go back all the way to the very beginning?
cried the disciple.

If you turn, you will not be going back, said Rabbi Boruch.
You will be standing beyond the last gate:
you will stand in faith.

Whitewater Rapids

ADAPTED BY MARC KAMINSKY AND STEVE ZEITLIN FROM
THE STORY "WHITEWATER" BY JEWISH RENEWAL MOVEMENT
COFOUNDER RABBI ZALMAN SCHACHTER-SHALOMI[27]

Aboard a rowboat, leisurely rowing
on a calm lake, requiring little maneuvering,
Shmuel asked Rabbi Nachman about free will.

Before he could answer,
the boat hit whitewater rapids,
and Shmuel, in a sweat, pulled his oars
to the left, to the right, straining,
barely missing boulders, tree stumps,
whirlpools. Finally, the boat hit
a two-foot waterfall, tumbled. Shmuel
released the oars and threw
his hands into the air. Miraculously,
they found themselves on smooth
waters again. Only then
did Rabbi Nachman answer.

On the glassy lake,
he said, *rowing was easy.*
But life is never so consistently calm.
On the waterfall, you were helpless.
You couldn't steer at all—the boat
was falling, careening, reeling.
Your fate was wholly in God's hands. But

in between the still waters
and the waterfall, on the whitewater
rapids, there's still room
for you to do some steering.

The Ring

ADAPTED BY MARC KAMINSKY AND STEVE
ZEITLIN FROM A TRADITIONAL TALE

Before the diagnosis of bipolar disorder brought extreme
and chaotic mood swings into the rigorous order
of a diagnostic concept, King Solomon suffered
manic moments of ecstasy cut short
by extended bouts of sadness.

To ease his anguish, he proclaimed that
whoever brought him a ring
that could make him sad when he was happy,
and happy when he was sad,
would win his daughter's hand in marriage.

Jewelers worked furiously, forging
rings of platinum, of silver, of gold, and of brass.
Children tried making rings woven of grass
with a flower tied atop—to no avail.

Then a jeweler's handsome son opened his grandmother's drawer
just as a beam of sunlight flashed
on the antique wedding ring she'd saved.

He carved some letters into the ring
and presented his gift to the king, who offered
the jeweler's son his daughter's hand
when he read the words engraved:
Gam Ze Ya'avor: This, too, shall pass.

COMMENTARY: The wise saying "This, too, shall pass" has been
my personal mantra ever since I heard the story of King Solomon
searching for a ring that would make "a sad man happy and a
happy man sad." This story serves to remind us that balance and
moderation are necessary parts of a Jewish way of life.

   During World War II, a ring engraved with "This, too, shall
pass"—or with the three Hebrew letters of the saying—became
popular among people in the military, and it can still be pur-
chased today. (Peninnah Schram)

The Beautiful Question

TRADITIONAL TALE RETOLD BY STEVE ZEITLIN

Why must a Jew
always answer a question with a question?

Because a good question is half the answer,

and because a shtetl student,
studying by candlelight,
screamed suddenly,
What is the meaning of life?

He ran to wake the rabbi in the middle of the night.
The rabbi smacked him.

You have such a beautiful question.
Why would you exchange it for an answer?

COMMENTARY: Jews are a people who question. They wrestle, as Jacob did with the angel—or was it with the Prophet Elijah? or with Esau? or with himself? Traditionally, the youngest person at the seder table is required to ask the four questions, because without those questions, the seder cannot proceed. Whenever people have asked me questions in my role as a Jewish storyteller, I, like other storytellers, respond with a story. Life itself proceeds by posing questions. (Peninnah Schram)

Lost in the Woods

TRADITIONAL TALE RETOLD BY PENINNAH SCHRAM

Shmuel wandered into the woods
and immediately found himself lost.
He wandered in and out of brambles,
overgrown branches, alone, hungry, frightened.

It grew dark, and he wandered blindly
through night, then day,
then an even darker night.

At last he came across another human being.
Thank God I found you, Shmuel said.
I have been lost for three days.

Three days, the man said.
I have been lost for three years.

Shmuel began to weep. *That is no good.*
Now I will never
find my way out of these woods.

It's true I cannot help you find the path
leading out of the woods, the man said.

But I can point you to the many paths
that will not *lead you out of the woods.*

Shmuel Discovers a Purpose in Life

TRADITIONAL TALE RETOLD BY RABBI EDWARD SCHECTER

Shmuel believes his life lacks purpose.
In his search for meaning,
he wanders into the woods
but finds himself lost, cold, fatigued.

Then he sees a light in the distance.

He approaches a cottage, peers into the window,
where he spots a blazing fireplace.

The door has been left open.
He steps inside, warms himself,
feels renewed, relieved.

Before he departs, he sees a sign above the door:

Be sure to throw a log
onto the fire
when you leave.

CODA

TRADITIONAL TALE RETOLD BY RABBI EDWARD SCHECTER

The next traveler comes to the cottage.
He sees the sign
but doesn't add a log to the fire when he leaves.

The traveler who follows finds only a darkened cabin.

Concerto

ADAPTED BY STEVE ZEITLIN FROM A TRADITIONAL
TALE RETOLD BY RABBI ELI RUBENSTEIN

As a concert
by Itzhak Perlman got underway,

a string on his violin snapped.
His playing came to a halt.

The crowd expected him to restring it.
Instead, he motioned to the conductor
to begin the movement again.

He played the full concerto
on only three strings—with no flaws.
The audience, awed by the magnificent strains,
rose in spontaneous applause.
He silenced them with a single phrase:

Our job is to make music
with what remains.

FINAL THOUGHTS

IN CLOSING, SOME LINES FROM EARLY IN THE BOOK COME BACK TO me—the Jews fled Egypt without enough time to allow their bread to rise. Jews have always been a "portable people," traveling from place to place—sometimes directed by God, other times by humans; sometimes escaping from dire straits, other times seeking a better life.

I realize now that my quest to transform Jewish jokes and stories into poems—and, more specifically, to miniaturize many Jewish stories and jokes from ancient times to the present into a poem no longer than a page, if not shorter—was to make them more portable, so Jews, a portable people, and all of us, can more easily carry them with us. After all, to paraphrase Peninnah Schram, what's lighter to carry than stories and poems in the heart?

In these 180 or so short-form poems I've tried to make portable so many of the things Jews past and present love(d) to talk about, obsess about, laugh about—the quintessential Jewish poetic imagination that could not be extinguished even during the Holocaust.

My wish is that, having experienced the poetry, philosophy, protest, and promise in these jewels of Jewish humor and storytelling, you will more deeply appreciate the endlessly rich and unique Jewish perspective on the world. I hope you will nestle in your consciousness and heart the vast range of tragedy and joy, mysticism and materialism, confoundment and wisdom that offers us all, Jews and non-Jews, a creative, engaged, joyful, and—ultimately—spiritual way of being in the world.

QUESTIONS FOR DISCUSSION

1. JEWels . . . *in Stories*

1. Introduction (p. xvii): Do you agree with Michael Gold that talk tends to be especially refreshing for Jews? Do Jews interrupt each other more often than other people do? If so, what in the Jewish tradition might give rise to a Jewish gift for gab?

2. Introduction (p. xvii): In our own day, when a great many means of communication are open to us, what makes oral tradition "an institution in Jewish religious learning as sacred as the written word"? Have memory and oral tradition become devalued when so much digital knowledge is at our fingertips?

3. "Now the Story" (p. 3): What does this poem say to you about Jewish memory, belief, and faith? How do you relate to the poem's ending, "And it was"?

4. "Stories" (p. 4): Peninnah Schram writes, "What has never been fully lost, stolen, or destroyed is learning—the wealth of stories, sacred and secular, that continue to be held as Jewish treasures." What makes a Jewish story, sacred or secular, a Jewish treasure? What Jewish stories do you treasure most and why?

5. "Tales" (p. 5): Peninnah Schram's commentary reflects on how her immigrant parents "told me very different kinds of stories. . . . From my mother's personal stories of pogroms and teaching tales, I learned how to behave and be a Jew. My father opened the path to wonder and curiosity through his stories and songs." What stories did your parents tell you? What messages or lessons did you find within them?

6. "Burning the Scrolls" (p. 7): The commentary presents various interpretations of the kabbalistic teaching that the Torah is "black fire on white fire": the black refers to the fiery letters and the white to the spaces between them; the letters are black fire set against the white fire of God's creation; "the black letters are limited, limiting, and fixed. The white spaces . . . catapult us into the realm of the limitless and the ever-changing, ever-growing. They are the silence, the song, the story." How do you understand this mystical image of the Torah?

7. "A Table with People" (p. 8): What does Marc Kaminsky's poem about a *tish mit mentshn*, "a table with people," evoke in you?

2. JEWels . . . *on a Journey*

1. Introduction (p. xvii): How do you understand that idea that "Jews have always been a 'portable people'"? To what extent does your life, or the life of Jews you know, feel portable today?

2. Introduction (p. xvii): David Arnow characterizes Abraham's journey at God's command as "test[ing] the strength of the two core qualities of hope . . . the willingness to embrace the possibility of a future fundamentally different than the present and the readiness to help bring it about." Have you embarked on a journey that feels close to this understanding of hope?

3. "Paradise" (p. 13): If you were to put on Shmuel's shoes that were turned around and returned to a home just like the one you left and found a spouse just like yours, would you be more likely to think, "every place is the same; get me out of here"? Or, might you think, "perhaps this *is* Paradise?"

4. "The Guru" (p. 15): What is the attraction of Buddhism for Jews? Are "Jewbus" looking for something as far away as possible from Jewish teachings and rituals, or are there deeper elements shared by the two religions?

5. "Mameloshen" (p. 17): Jews understand the word *mensch* to mean a good person. According to some sources, the word *mensch* derives from Cicero's concept of *humanitas*, which was literally translated as *Menschlichkeit* in Yiddish. Does this mean that all who are part of humankind can aspire to menschhood?

6. "Bubba Truth" (p. 19): When Bubba Truth says "tell them I *was* young and beautiful," is she lying or telling the truth? Is she playing a trick on time? After all, she could have said, "tell them I *am* young and beautiful."

7. "Traveler's Prayer" (p. 20): How do you calculate the risks you face when you leave your home for a journey? How can you be sure you will return, and your home will be there as it was when you left? What journeys did you embark upon with the greatest risk of either not getting to the place you were going or not ever returning home?

3. JEWels . . . *from the Old Country*

1. "The Magic Ship" (p. 25): Does Rabbi Shimon's escape strike you as a magic trick or a miracle? What do you think of the suggestion in the commentary that things that we ourselves experience can be considered miracles, but when they happen to others—magic? What miracles and/or magic have touched your life?

2. "Once Upon a Time in the Old Country" (p. 33): The cask of wine that turns out to be a cask of water suggests metaphorically that when a person shirks responsibilities to a task or a cause, others may do the same. Have you ever been in this situation? Is it wise to think, "If I don't do it, perhaps no one else will either?"

3. "The Hunchback" (p. 35): When faced with a choice—either he or his would-be bride will become a hunchback—the hunchback says, "Let it be me." Would you have made that choice? Have you ever wished that you yourself could take on another person's suffering?

4. "An Offspring's Answer" (p. 39): How might this child's imagined decision to "fly . . . her own [future] children across the sea" instead of caring for her elderly parent apply to your parents and/or your children?

5. "Elijah" (p. 45): What ideas or teachings might be gleaned from this story of a writer visiting a seder in search of the prophet Elijah who is then himself mistaken for Elijah?

6. "The Hasid" (p. 48): In this joke-poem, the Hasid is told to put out a fire by engaging in seemingly senseless rituals—but then he is also told to throw water. Can prayer and ritual also be pragmatic responses to crises? Have you ever combined ritual and prayer with more concrete problem solving?

7. "The Rooster Prince" (p. 53): Is the protagonist's solution to the young prince's rooster problem advice you've ever needed to follow in your life?

4. JEWels ... *in Jokes*

1. Introduction (p. xvii): The author postulates that Jewish humor is different from all other kinds of humor because of "talmudic reasoning" or convoluted logic as well as Jews' predilections to frame their jokes as questions. What do you think makes Jewish humor distinctive?

2. "The Perfect Girl" (p. 80): Is the search for perfection in a love relationship doomed? Can one's ideals guide one's search for a soulmate?

3. "Toyota" (p. 88): The commentary reflects on how this bit of dark humor broke the ice in the dismal days after the author's mother passed away. Has black humor ever helped you deal with a miserable situation?

4. "The Summum Bonum" (p. 91): Under what, if any, circumstances might the joys of Jewish ritual and the pleasures of sex be considered equivalent valences of sacred experience?

5. "Twenty Years" (p. 97): Beyond the laugh, here lies a question: Would you be happy to give part of your life in order to extend the life of a loved one?

6. "Seven Differences between a Joke and a Poem" (p. 98): How would you characterize the differences between a joke and a poem? Does presenting jokes in poetic form, the crux of this chapter, bring out philosophical or other qualities embedded in the humor?

7. "Optimism/Pessimism" (p. 99): Do you agree with the poet's characterization of optimists and pessimists? Do you consider yourself an optimist or a pessimist, and why?

5. JEWels . . . *from Torah*

1. Introduction (p. xvii): Rabbi Lawrence Kushner says that each of us has an innermost teaching, "a Torah, unique to that person. . . . Some seem to know their Torahs very early in life and speak and sing them in a myriad of ways. Others spend their whole lives stammering, shaping, and rehearsing them." How do you understand this metaphor? Would you say you knew your Torah early in life or you have spent much of your life "stammering, shaping, and rehearsing" it?

2. "The *Tsimtsum*" (p. 103): Do you agree with Rabbi Edward Schecter's appraisement, "The universe / springs forth from the dark, / leaving a spark / of divinity in everything"? Is there a spark of divinity in everything, even in evil, in the world?

3. "Rabbi Simon Said" (p. 104): Whose position on the creation of human beings most resembles your own: Lovingkindness's, Truth's, Justice's, Peace's, God's? Why?

4. "What I Would Tell Adam and Eve" (p. 106): What do you think poet Francine Witte is really saying here? What would you tell Adam and Eve if you could?

5. "The Birth of Memory" (p. 109): Peninnah Schram's commentary quotes cognitive psychologist Roger Schank: "We need to tell someone else a story that describes our experiences because the process of creating the story also creates the memory structure that will contain the gist of the story for the rest of our lives. Talking is remembering." Is Schank saying that talking is the same as remembering? When you think of oft-repeated recollections in your life, does the original event or the story about it seem most alive to you?

6. "Moses and the Superhero" (p. 113): Is Moses the ultimate biblical superhero? Is Superman the ultimate comic superhero? Who is a superhero to you and why?

7. "Miriam's Wandering Well" (p. 117): Why would modern Jews still need Miriam's wandering well?

6. JEWels . . . *Shaped by the Holocaust*

1. Introduction (p. xvii): Anne Frank writes that she keeps her ideals "because in spite of everything I still believe that people are really good at heart." Do you believe this about humanity?

2. "Tickling the Corpse" (p. 125): The author suggests that given the Holocaust, "laughter is an act of faith." Do you agree?

3. "Holocaust Jokes" (p. 126): Do you agree with the "comedian" that God wasn't there during the Holocaust?

4. "Riding with the Moon" (p. 129): The commentary elucidates how storyteller Roslyn Bresnick-Perry told this among many other stories about her cousin Zisl to help her cope with an unfathomable loss. Has sharing stories, poems, artwork, or another creative art form helped you come to terms with a deep loss?

5. "Hovering above the Pit" (p. 132): In this story the Rabbi flies across the pit, relying on his faith and the merit of his ancestors. Can you think of other situations in imagined or real life in which faith or love enables the protagonist to take an impossible jump, landing safely on the other side?

6. "The Twig" (p. 137): Renée Fodor Schwarz wrote her poetry with a twig in the sand outside her barracks and covered it up to avoid discovery. What value do you think ephemeral art would have had for her and other inmates who created it?

7. "In Memory of Those Who Died in Vain in the Holocaust" (p. 138): Beginning with "In memory of . . . ," what would you add to Renée Fodor Schwarz's poem (excerpted here)?

8. "Forgotten Acts of Courage" (p. 139): Have you or has someone you know taken the fraught risk to "step out of line"? What happened? Are there other undertakings in your life that you would assess as "forgotten act[s] of courage"?

9. "Death Train" (p. 143): Do you believe, as the protagonist Ernie counsels, that when interacting with children in the darkest of times, *"there is no room for truth here"*?

7. JEWels . . . in Glimpses of Jewish American Lives

1. "Rummage" (p. 149): In your family, are there objects or mementos brought from the Old Country or handed down through the generations? Do you have any of these in your home? How are they displayed?

2. "Jewish and Goyish" (p. 159): In this famous monologue, Lenny Bruce can be seen as poking fun at the Jewish propensity to categorize everything in the world as either Jewish (e.g., pumpernickel bread, black cherry soda, maca-roons) or non-Jewish (e.g., white bread, trailer parks, Drake's cakes). What would you categorize as definitely Jewish—or non-Jewish?

3. "Reflection" (p. 164): What do you think Zev's father was referring to when he introduced Zev to the doctor by saying, "That's my son; I used to be him"? In what, if any, ways might one of your parents say that about you? Could you say that about your own children?

4. "To Kvell or Not to Kvell" (p. 166): This poem revels in Yiddish words like *kvelling* and *nachas*. Are there Yiddish phrases or expressions that you relish in conversation?

5. "The Driver Said" (p. 169): The author submits that poet Robert Hershon's sug-gestion that a real neighborhood is where the butcher comes to your funeral provides a definition for community. What characteristics constitute a vibrant community for you?

6. "Sally" (p. 173): This poem suggests that Sally, putting on makeup in the mirror on her last night on earth, was totally herself when she died. What would it mean to you to be totally yourself at the end of life?

7. "Abraham Joshua Heschel Goes to Selma" (p. 177): The author quotes Rabbi Abraham Joshua Heschel as saying, "*In a free society some are guilty, but all are responsible.*" What does this statement mean to you? What do you feel responsible for?

8. JEWels . . . *in Jewish Foods*

1. Introduction (p. xvii): What Jewish dishes does your family relish? Are they part of holiday celebrations? Are there stories connected to them?

2. "Happiness" (p. 184): For baker Moishe Sacks, his weekly routine—"Tuesday strudel, Wednesday babkas"—brought him happiness. What daily life or work routines bring you joy?

3. "The Atheist" (p. 186): Friends of the author, Simon Lichman and Rivanna Miller, who live in Jerusalem bring Jewish and Palestinian schoolchildren together to make pickles. They believe there are so many different ways of making pickles that it serves as a way of breaking the ice, starting conversations, and often getting the families of the children talking and laughing. Have you ever shared foods that are part of your culture with people from other cultures? What was it like?

4. "The Jewish Waiter" (p. 188): Often set in Katz's, the Carnegie, the 2nd Avenue Deli, or Jewish delis in American cities other than New York, jokes about the Jewish delicatessen experience abound. This poem gathers a couple of them—"Who ordered the clean glass?"; "Is anything alright?" Can you think of other Jewish jokes set in Jewish delis? What are these jokes really about?

5. "How to Make Blintzes" (p. 193): A friend told the author that he heard his rabbi tell this story as part of a sermon. The rabbi intended it as a parable about the need to do things right: If you skimp on key elements of, say, a bar mitzvah, it won't really be a bar mitzvah. What does this story say to you about the need to implement traditions and rituals fully?

6. "2nd Avenue Kosher" (p. 194): In our increasingly multicultural society, we often find ourselves mixing and matching foods. What cuisines do you find yourself combining for home cooking or take out? Does this mingling of dishes have significance beyond the relishing of a good meal?

7. "From 'The Whole Soul'" (p. 196): Do you relate to Philip Levine's likening of the soul to an onion with its many layers? Many cultures speak of opening a window when a person is dying to allow the soul to "fly" out like a bird. What metaphors for the soul in literature, film, or you own life speak to you?

9. JEWels . . . *in Conversations with God*

1. Introduction (p. xvii): Which of the many ways Jews can relate to God as offered here comes closest to your own personal worldview?

2. "The Messiah #1" (p. 199): In this poem, inspired from Michael Gold's *Jews without Money*, the speaker observes, "We had no Santa Claus, but we had a Messiah." Playfully consider some of the differences.

3. "Tevye the Milkman Said" (p. 207): Consider Rabbi Dr. Yaakov Brawer's riff on Tevye's famous question, "Would it spoil some vast eternal plan if I were a wealthy man?" Do you think, as Brawer suggests, the universe would have to be reconstructed to accommodate such a change?

4. "A Pair of Pants" (p. 210): What does it say about Jews that they can poke fun at the sacred, God included, in their humor?

5. "The DNA in My Coffee—A True Story" (p. 212): What do you think of Lisa Lipkin's dad's perspectives: "*To me, God is the sum total of all the intelligence in the universe*"; "*Faith, kiddo, is anything where the evidence is missing*"; and, when asked what his Jewish background means to him, "*somehow humankind still has potential for goodness*"?

6. "Six Lines" (p. 216): What might Aaron Zeitlin mean by "Only what is hopeless on this earth has beauty, and only the ephemeral is godly"? Are there ephemeral rituals or moments that feel sacred and beautiful to you?

7. "Lifeline" (p. 218): What does this poem suggest about the tasks you yourself might wish to undertake in the world?

10. JEWels . . . *on the Meaning of Life*

1. Introduction (p. xvii): Rabbi Edward Schecter speaks of Moses passing on God's charge to the Jewish people: "Choose life." Does this message resonate in the choices you or people you know have made?

2. "The Razbash on Old Age" (p. 235): How do you relate to the idea, "When you die, everything you learned searches for a new learner, but everything you did not learn ceases to exist for eternity"?

3. "Doctor, Doctor" (p. 236): This joke begs another question: Is it more important to live a long life or to pack rich experiences into a shorter time?

4. "The Razbash on Forgiveness" (p. 238): This poem cites a talmudic teaching, *"The agony of dying is atonement enough,"* to suggest that God will forgive each of us on our deathbeds even if we have not confessed our sins in life. Do you think that "dying is atonement enough"?

5. "The Fiftieth Gate" (p. 243): Rabbi Boruch of Medzhybizh suggests that every question posed by humankind is a gate to be opened, and when a life traveler finally comes upon a question no human being has ever answered, the traveler needs to stand *"in faith."* Do you feel that faith is a way forward when we confront unanswerable questions?

6. "Whitewater Rapids" (p. 244): How have you managed to navigate the tension between acceptance (a boat going over a waterfall) and "do[ing] some steering" in rough waters?

7. "Concerto" (p. 249): Have you sought to do what Itzhak Perlman teaches, *"Our job is to make music with what remains"*?

SOURCE ACKNOWLEDGMENTS

"It Is Raining on the House of Anne Frank" and "A Short History of Judaic Thought in the Twentieth Century," by Linda Pastan, originally appeared in *The Five Stages of Grief* (New York: Norton, 1978). © 1978 by Linda Pastan. Used by permission of W. W. Norton & Company, Inc. Used by permission of Linda Pastan in care of the Jean V. Naggar Literary Agency, Inc. (permissions@jvnla.com).

"Rachel," by Linda Pastan, originally appeared in *Aspects of Eve*. © 1970, 1971, 1972, 1973, 1974, 1975 by Linda Pastan. Used by permission of Liveright Publishing Corporation.

"Kaddish in the Boxcar of Death" and "Closer," written by Aaron Zeitlin and translated by Morris M. Faierstein, originally appeared in *Poems of the Holocaust and Poems of Faith*, edited by Morris M. Faierstein (iUniverse, 2007).

"The Bagel," by David Ignatow, originally appeared in *Against the Evidence: Selected Poems, 1934–1994* (Hanover NH: Wesleyan University Press, 1994). © 1993 by David Ignatow. Used by permission.

"The Whole Soul," by Philip Levine, originally appeared in *Poetry* (December 1986): 131–32.

"God and DNA over Coffee" by Lisa Lipkin, originally appeared in *Forward*, http://storystrategies.net/coffee.pdf.

"Six Lines" by Aaron Zeitlin and translated from the Yiddish by Robert Friend. Translation copyright © Jean Shapiro Cantu.

"Time All at Once," by Caroline Harris, originally appeared in *Voices: The Journal of New York Folklore* 46, no. 1–2 (Spring–Summer 2020): 22–25.

"The Kiss," by Mark Solomon, originally appeared in *My True Body* (New York: Havel Havulim, 2016).

NOTES

INTRODUCTION

1. Schwartz, *Tree of Souls*, 85–86. Among his sources for this story cycle, Schwartz cites *Genesis Rabbah* 31:11 and *Bava Batra* 16b.
2. Schwartz, *Tree of Souls*, 87.
3. Scheub, *Poem in the Story*, 23.
4. Novak and Waldoks, *The Big Book of Jewish Humor*, xviii.
5. Irving Kristol, "Is Jewish Humor Dead?: The Rise and Fall of the Jewish Joke," *Commentary* 12 (November 1951): 432.
6. Personal communication with Zev Shanken, January 2021.
7. Kravitz and Olitzky, *Pirke Avot* 5:15, 84.
8. Schwartz, *Circle Spinning*, 3.

1. IN STORIES

1. Gold, *Jews without Money*, 112–13.
2. Kirshenblatt-Gimblett, *Traditional Storytelling in the Toronto Jewish Community*, 1, 62.
3. Wiesel, *Gates of the Forest*, 1.
4. Zeitlin, *Because God Loves Stories*, 24.
5. Wiesel, *Sages and Dreamers*, 79.
6. Wiesel, *Gates of the Forest*, 1.
7. Sam Roberts, "Edgar Hilsenrath, 92, Writer of Unvarnished Holocaust Novels, Dies," *New York Times*, January 4, 2019.
8. Wiesel, *Souls on Fire*, 2.
9. See Schwartz, *Tree of Souls*, 177.
10. Schram, *Chosen Tales*, xv–xxxiii. See foreword by Rabbi Avraham Weiss.
11. See Kaminsky, *A Table with People*, 84.

2. ON A JOURNEY

1. Arnow, *Choosing Hope*, 49.
2. See, for example, Ausubel, *A Treasury of Jewish Folklore*, 334–36.
3. Simon, *Wise Men of Helm and Their Merry Tales*, 88–102.
4. Kravitz and Olitzky, *Pirke Avot*, 109.
5. See Sigalow, *American JewBu*.
6. Yolen, *Favorite Folktales from around the World*, 3–4.
7. "Traveler's Prayer" appears in the prayerbooks Teutsch, *Kol Haneshamah*, 174, and Aigen, *Hadesh Yameinu—Renew Our Days*, 656.

3. FROM THE OLD COUNTRY

1. Samuel, *Little Did I Know*, 26.

2. From the author's conversation with Rabbi Edward Schecter, November 2018.

3. Zborowski and Herzog, *Life Is with People*, ix–xviii.

4. From the author's interview with Cherie Karo Schwartz, April 1995.

5. From the story "Rabbi Shimon's Escape," in Schwartz, *Gabriel's Palace*, 126–27. In a note (309), Schwartz writes that the traditional tale was "collected by Max Grunwald from an unknown teller in the Balkans."

6. Kushner, *Book of Letters*, 13.

7. See Schwartz, *Tree of Souls*, 281–82.

8. This story is credited to the third-century talmudist, halakhist, and aggadist Rabbi Hanina Bar Hama.

9. From the author's interview with Rabbi David Holtz, September 20, 1995. This story also appears in Schram, *Jewish Stories One Generation Tells Another*, 478–81.

10. Zev Shanken and the present author heard versions of this story told on different occasions. The tale also appears in Schram, *Stories within Stories*, 78–81, and Schram and Sasso, *Jewish Stories of Love and Marriage*, 63–64. "A Match Made in Heaven" is the title in both of the cited books.

11. From the author's interview with Sylvia Cole, May 1995.

12. Hameln, *Memoirs of Glückel of Hameln*, 2–3.

13. Hameln, *Memoirs of Glückel of Hameln*, 2–3.

14. From the author's interview with Rabbi David Holtz at Temple Beth Abraham, Tarrytown, New York, September 20, 1995. This story also appears as "The Mountain and the Cliff" in Schram, *Chosen Tales*, 161–65.

15. See Faust's full poem and painting in Hufford, Hunt, and Zeitlin, *Grand Generation*, 59.

16. Hufford, Hunt, and Zeitlin, *Grand Generation*, 59.

17. See, for example, Jaffe and Zeitlin, *While Standing on One Foot*, 66–69; Oberman, *Solomon and the Ant*, 107–10; Rossel, *Essential Jewish Stories*, 116–17.

18. Dov Noy (1920–2013) was a renowned folklorist and ethnologist. Born on October 20, 1920, in Kolomyya, Poland (now Ukraine), he later immigrated to Palestine, where he began his academic studies at the Hebrew University of Jerusalem. He obtained his doctorate in folklore from Indiana University in 1954 with a dissertation on the motif-index of Talmudic-Midrashic tales (under the name Dov Neuman). In 1955 he founded the Israel Folktale Archives at the University of Haifa.

19. From the author's interview with Jack Tepper, August 31, 1990.

20. From an interview with Baruch Lumet for the American Jewish Committee's William E. Wiener Oral History Library, December 12, 1976.

21. Buber, *Tales of the Hasidim*, 70.

22. Ausubel, *Treasury of Jewish Folklore*, 323.

23. See Schram, "The Rooster Who Would Be King," in *Jewish Stories One Generation Tells Another*, 292–95, and "The Prince Who Thought He Was a Rooster," in Schwartz, *Palace of Pearls*, 186–88.

24. The Nachman version of this story appears as "The Prince Who Thought He Was a Rooster," in Schwartz, *A Palace of Pearls*, 186–87. The quote about teachers in the commentary is on 188.

25. Wiesel, *Souls on Fire*, 232.

26. Wiesel, *Souls on Fire*, 232.

27. Ueland, *If You Want to Write*, 26.

28. Rabbi Edward Schecter heard this story at one of Elie Wiesel's talks at the 92nd Street Y and used it in his sermon on Rosh Hashanah morning, 1981. See "A Remembered Story," in Schram, *Stories within Stories*, 252–55. See also "The Forgotten Story," in Frankel, *Classic Tales*, 485–89.

29. See Peretz, *I. L. Peretz Reader*, 146–51. Peretz's short story "Bontshe Shvayg" ("Bontshe the Silent") was first published in 1894.

30. See Kirshenblatt and Kirshenblatt-Gimblett, *They Called Me Mayer July*, 3, 13, 23, 29, 35, 123, 127, 199, 252.

4. IN JOKES

1. See Zeitlin, *Because God Loves Stories*, 255.

2. For example, Nancy Maxwell, Bob Mankoff, Ruth Wisse, Moshe Waldoks.

3. Leo Rosten, Letter to the Editor, *New York Times*, January 27, 1991.

4. Kravitz and Olitzky, *Pirke Avot*, 1.14, 10.

5. Stein, *Fiddler on the Roof*.

6. "A Portrait of Jewish Americans: Findings from a Pew Research Study of American Jews," Pew Research Center, October 1, 2013, https://www.pewresearch.org/wp-content/uploads/sites/7/2013/10/jewish-american-full-report-for-web.pdf.

7. Herb Shore, "'A String from Pearls' and Other Gems" (unpublished manuscript), 74.

8. From the author's interview with Jack Tepper, August 31, 1990.

9. Gimbel, *Isn't That Clever*, 3.

10. Adapted from Cohen, *Jewish Wry*, 16.

11. D. W. Black, "Laughter," *Journal of the American Medical Association* 252, no. 21 (December 7, 1984): 2995–98.

12. "2 Experts, Scientific and Wry, Study Laughter," *New York Times*, December 9, 1984, https://www.nytimes.com/1984/12/09/us/2-experts-scientific-and-wry-study-laughter.html.

13. See, for example, Herb Shore, "'A Yellow Rose from Texas' without Thorns" (unpublished manuscript, Dallas: Community Homes for Adults, 1999), 22.

14. Ausubel, *Treasury of Jewish Folklore*, 3.

15. "Mrs. Meir Says Moses Made Israel Oil-Poor," *New York Times*, June 11, 1973.

16. "Selected Quotes from Golda Meir," Metropolitan State University of Denver, Golda Meir Center for Leadership.

17. From the author's interview with Rubin Levine, May 1995.

18. Abe Lass also told this tale on WNYC's *Senior Edition*. Lass's collection of dirty Yiddish jokes on cassette tape are housed in City Lore's audiotape archives.

19. Howe, *World of Our Fathers*, 488.

20. From the author's interview with Abe Lass, City Lore, New York City, November 14, 1993.

21. To learn more about Sparrow, see Sparrow, *America*.

22. See Sweeney, *If It's Not One Thing, It's Your Mother*. Sometimes the phrase is also attributed to *Saturday Night Live* comedian Gilda Radner.

23. See, for example, Herb Shore, "A Breast from Chicken and Other Morsels" (unpublished manuscript, Dallas: Adventure Graphics, 1994), 63.

24. Arnow, *Choosing Hope*, 196.

5. FROM TORAH

1. Kushner, *God Was in This Place and I, I Did Not Know*, 168.

2. See Schwartz, *Tree of Souls*, xliv–xlviii.

3. Schwartz, *Tree of Souls*, 14.

4. See Schwartz, *Tree of Souls*, 14.

5. See Schwartz, *Tree of Souls*, 124.

6. Albeck and Theodor, *Bereschit Rabba*, 8:5, 60; Freedman and Simon, *Midrash Rabbah: Genesis*, 1:58. The midrash appears in Ornstein, *Cain v. Abel*, xxiii.

7. Schwartz, *Tree of Souls*, 405.

8. Schank, *Tell Me a Story*, 115.

9. Rosten, *Joys of Yiddish*, xv.

10. Schwartz, *Tree of Souls*, 301–2.

11. See Schwartz, *Gabriel's Palace*, 250–51; Rabbi Tamara Cohen, "Miriam's Cup: A Modern Feminist Symbol," https://www.myjewishlearning.com/article/miriams-cup/. See also Numbers 20:1.

12. See Schwartz, *Tree of Souls*, 39, 416.

13. Schram, *Chosen Tales*, 363.

14. Mary Regina Morrell, "Hidden Saints: Legends of the Lamed Vavniks," *Vermont Catholic*, September 22, 2020, https://vermontcatholic.org/uncategorized/hidden-saints-the-legend-of-the-lamed-vavniks/.

15. See Schram, *Chosen Tales*, 363.

16. Siegel, *Radiance*, 196.

6. SHAPED BY THE HOLOCAUST

1. Eliach, *Hasidic Tales of the Holocaust*, xvii.

2. See Douglas Martin, "Germaine Tillion, French Anthropologist and Resistance Figure, Dies at 100," *New York Times*, April 25, 2008.

3. Frank, *Diary of a Young Girl*, 278.

4. Eliach, *Hasidic Tales of the Holocaust*, xix–xx.

5. Pastan, *Five Stages of Grief*, 21.

6. See Bresnick-Perry, *I Loved My Mother on Saturdays*, 40–46.

7. Bresnick-Perry, *I Loved My Mother on Saturdays*, 25.

8. Gutterman and Shalev, *To Bear Witness*, 176–78.

9. Oren Dagan, "Yehuda Maimon, Krakow Ghetto Fighter, Dies at 96," *Davar*, May 12, 2020, https://en.davar1.co.il/266188/.

10. Eliach, *Hasidic Tales of the Holocaust*, 3–4.

11. Eliach, *Hasidic Tales of the Holocaust*, 151–53.

12. Schwartz, *Renée*, 107.

13. Schwartz, *Renée*, 143–47.

14. Rachel Yang, "In Inspiring Emmys Speech, Alex Borstein Tells Women to 'Step Out of Line,'" *Entertainment Weekly*, September 23, 2013, https://ew.com/emmys/2019/09/23/emmys-speech-alex-borstein-tells-women-step-out-of-line/.

15. Pastan, *Aspects of Eve*, 3.

16. Schwartz-Bart, *Last of the Just*, 373.

17. Holloway, *Waiting for the Last Bus*, 101.

18. Zeitlin, *Poems of the Holocaust and Poems of Faith*, 12.

7. IN GLIMPSES OF JEWISH AMERICAN LIFE

1. Kaminsky and Supraner, *Daily Bread*, 41.

2. Alter Yisrael Shimon Feuerman, "The Healing Power of Jokes," *Tablet*, June 12, 2019, https://www.tabletmag.com/sections/community/articles/the-healing-power-of-jokes.

3. Sirowitz, *Mother Said*, 19.

4. Pastan, *Five Stages of Grief*, 24.

5. This Lenny Bruce routine is sometimes referred to as "Jewish-Goyish." After being performed in November 1961 at the Curran Theatre in San Francisco, a version was published in *Playboy* magazine and has been republished countless times since.

6. Lenny Bruce, "Jewish and Goyish," https://www.myjewishlearning.com/article/jewish-and-goyish/.

7. A variation of the chicken joke appears in Woody Allen's 1977 film *Annie Hall*.

8. Solomon, *My True Body*, 27.

9. Hershon, *How to Ride on the Woodlawn Express*, 16.

10. See Kugelmass, *Miracle on Intervale Avenue*, 76.

11. See Kaplan, *Abraham Joshua Heschel*. See also Susannah Heschel, "Theological Affinities in the Writings of Abraham Joshua Heschel and Martin Luther King, Jr.," The Rabbinical Assembly, https://www.rabbinicalassembly.org/sites/default/files/public /resources-ideas/cj/classics/heschel/theological-affinities-in-the-writings-o.pdf.

12. Abraham Joshua Heschel, "Religion and Race," Voices of Democracy, January 14, 1963, https://voicesofdemocracy.umd.edu/heschel-religion-and-race-speech-text/.

8. IN JEWISH FOODS

1. Jodi Kantor, "A History of the Mideast in the Humble Chickpea," *New York Times*, July 10, 2002, https://www.nytimes.com/2002/07/10/dining/a-history-of-the -mideast-in-the-humble-chickpea.html.

2. Dene Mullen, "Does Egypt Have the Best Falafel in the World?," BBC, July 16, 2019, https://www.bbc.com/travel/article/20190715-does-egypt-have-the-best -falafel-in-the-world.

3. Maria Godoy, "Beans and Rice for Passover? A Divisive Question Gets the Rabbis' Okay," NPR, April 23, 2016, https://www.npr.org/sections/thesalt/2016/04/23 /475266363/beans-and-rice-for-passover-a-divisive-question-gets-the-rabbis-ok.

4. Wex, *Rhapsody in Schmaltz*, 256.

5. Ignatow, *Against the Evidence*, 62.

6. Zeiger, *Way to Castle Garden*, 7.

7. See Zeitlin, *Because God Loves Stories*, 178–81.

8. Moishe Sacks makes these observations in *The Grand Generation*, a documentary produced and directed by Paul Wagner, Marjorie Hunt, and Steve Zeitlin, 1993.

9. Umansky and Ashton, *Four Centuries of Jewish Women's Spirituality*, 55.

10. Weissler, *Voices of the Matriarchs*, 55.

11. The Bowery Boys, "The Pickle Civil War!," February 14, 2008, Bowery Boys New York City History, https://www.boweryboyshistory.com/2008/02/pickle-civil-war.html.

12. Adapted from a version in Ausubel, *A Treasury of Jewish Folklore*, 347.

13. Bernstein and Lehrer, *Five Oceans in a Teaspoon*, 62.

14. Excerpted from Levine, "The Whole Soul," *Poetry*, December 1986.

9. IN CONVERSATIONS WITH GOD

1. Baeck, *This People Israel*, 8.

2. Wiesel, *Souls on Fire*, 62.

3. Davidman and Tenenbaum, *Feminist Perspectives on Jewish Studies*, 76.

4. Heschel, *Ineffable Name of God*, epigraph.

5. Kaufman, *Critique of Religion and Philosophy*, 278.

6. Midrash Tehillim 123:2 on Isa. 43:12.

7. Gold, *Jews without Money*, 183–84.

8. Zeitlin, *Poems of the Holocaust and Poems of Faith*, 125.

9. See Schwartz, *Tree of Souls*, 492–95, 500, 519.

10. Sholem Aleichem, *Tevye the Dairyman and the Railroad Stories*, 13.

11. Yaakov Brawer, "Tevye's Query," Chabad.org, https://www.chabad.org/library /article_cdo/aid/3036/jewish/Tevyes-Query.htm.

12. Adapted from "He Should Have Taken More Time," Ausubel, *Treasury of Jewish Folklore*, 16.

13. Lisa Lipkin, "God and DNA over Coffee," *Forward*, http://storystrategies.net /coffee.pdf.

14. Weiss, "Black Fire on White Fire: The Power of Story," in Schram, *Chosen Tales*, xxvii–xxviii.

15. Havel, *Disturbing the Peace*, 88.

16. See, for example, Davis and Renov, *Happiness Guaranteed or Your Misery Back*, 291.

10. ON THE MEANING OF LIFE

1. Kravitz and Olitzky, *Pirke Avot*, 2:16, 30.

2. Heschel, "Death as Homecoming," 59.

3. See Baker, *Days of Sorrow and Pain*, 1.

4. Lloyd, *What Folklorists Do*, 156.

5. Ginsburg, "Foreword," in Schwartz, *Tree of Souls*, xvii.

6. Thomas Friedman, "Solving the Korea Crisis by Teaching a Horse to Sing," *New York Times*, June 14, 2017, https://www.nytimes.com/2017/06/14/opinion/north -korea-crisis-foreign-policy.html.

7. See Matt Axelrod, "Hineni: A Prayer for the Ability to Pray," MyJewishLearning .com, https://www.myjewishlearning.com/article/hineni-a-prayer-for-the -ability-to-pray/.

8. See Schwartz, *Tree of Souls*, 208.

9. See Schwartz, *Judaism and Vegetarianism*, 62.

10. Adapted from I. L. Peretz, "If Not Higher!," Yiddish Book Center's Great Jew- ish Books Teacher Resources, http://teachgreatjewishbooks.org/1-short-story -excerpt-i-l-peretzs-if-not-higher-1900-english-translation-ken-frieden-2011-and.

11. Harris, "Time All at Once," 22–25.

12. The Anne Roiphe comment appears in Kravitz and Olitzky, *Pirke Avot*, 108–9.

13. Frankl, *Man's Search for Meaning*, 120.

14. Schwartz, *Tree of Souls*, 203.

15. Schwartz, *Tree of Souls*, 204.

16. Seth Rogovoy, "The Secret Jewish History of Star Wars," *Forward*, December 16, 2015, https://forward.com/culture/327265/the-secret-jewish-history-of-star -wars/.

17. Schram, *Chosen Tales*, 5.

18. See Learsi, *Filled with Laughter*, 134.

19. Woody Allen popularized a variation of this traditional joke in the 1977 movie *Annie Hall*.

20. Doris Kirshenblatt's version of this traditional joke appears in Hufford, Hunt, and Zeitlin, *Grand Generation*, 29.

21. Scherman, *Complete ArtScroll Siddur*, 976.

22. Moishe Sacks made these observations in *The Grand Generation*, a 1993 documentary produced and directed by Paul Wagner, Marjorie Hunt, and Steve Zeitlin.

23. See Horn, *World to Come*, 24.

24. Wiesel, *Souls on Fire*, 199–200.

25. Wiesel, *Souls on Fire*, 199–200.

26. Buber, *Tales of the Hasidim*, 92.

27. Zalman Schachter-Shalomi's story "Whitewater" appears in Milgram and Frankel, *Mitzvah Stories*, 281–87.

BIBLIOGRAPHY

Aigen, Ronald S., ed. *Hadesh Yameinu/Renew Our Days: A Book of Jewish Prayer and Meditation*. Quebec, Canada: Congregation Dorshei Emet, 1996.

Albeck, Chanoch, and J. Theodor. *Bereschit Rabba*. Delhi, India: Facsimile, 2015.

Arnow, David. *Choosing Hope: The Heritage of Judaism*. Philadelphia: Jewish Publication Society, 2022.

Ausubel, Nathan. *A Treasury of Jewish Folklore*. New York: Crown, 1975.

Baeck, Leo. *This People Israel: The Meaning of Jewish Existence*. Philadelphia: Jewish Publication Society of America, 1964.

Baker, Leonard. *Days of Sorrow and Pain: Leo Baeck and the Berlin Jews*. New York: Macmillan, 1978.

Bernstein, Dennis, and Warren Lehrer. *Five Oceans in a Teaspoon*. Guttenberg NJ: Paper Crown, 2019.

Bresnick-Perry, Roslyn. *I Loved My Mother on Saturdays and Other Tales from the Shtetl and Beyond*. Teaneck NJ: Ben Yehuda, 2009.

Buber, Martin. *Tales of the Hasidim*. New York: Schocken, 1975.

Cohen, Sarah Blacher, ed. *Jewish Wry*. Detroit MI: Wayne State University Press, 1987.

Davidman, Lynn, and Shelly Tenenbaum. *Feminist Perspectives on Jewish Studies*. New Haven CT: Yale University Press, 1996

Davis, J. Morton, and Ruki D. Renov. *Happiness Guaranteed or Your Misery Back*. New York: Page, 2018.

Eliach, Yaffa. *Hasidic Tales of the Holocaust*. New York: Oxford University Press, 1982.

Frank, Anne. *Anne Frank: The Diary of a Young Girl*. Translated by B. M. Mooyaart-Doubleday. New York: Random House, 1952.

Frankel, Ellen. *The Classic Tales*. Lanham MD: Rowman & Littlefield, 1993.

Frankl, Viktor. *Man's Search for Meaning*. Boston: Beacon, 2006.

Freedman, H., and Maurice Simon. *Midrash Rabbah: Genesis, Volume 1*. London: Soncino, 1939.

Gimbel, Steven. *Isn't That Clever: A Philosophical Account of Humor and Comedy*. Oxfordshire, England: Routledge, 2020.

Ginsberg, Louis. *The Legends of the Jews: All Four Volumes–Complete*. Translated by Henrietta Szold. Philadelphia: Jewish Publication Society, 1909.

Gold, Michael. *Jews without Money*. New York: Horace Liveright, 2004.

Gutterman, Bella, and Avner Shalev. *To Bear Witness: Holocaust Remembrance at Yad Vashem*. Jerusalem: Yad Vashem, 2005.

Hameln, Glückel of. *The Memoirs of Glückel of Hameln*. Translated by Marvin Lowenthal. New York: Schocken, 1977.

Harris, Caroline. "Time All at Once." *Voices: The Journal of New York Folklore* 46, nos. 1–2 (Spring–Summer 2020): 22–25.

Havel, Vaclav. *Disturbing the Peace: A Conversation with Karel Huizdala*. New York: Vintage, 1991.

Hershon, Robert. *How to Ride on the Woodlawn Express*. New York: Sun, 1985.

Heschel, Abraham J. "Death as Homecoming." In *Jewish Reflections on Death*, edited by Jack Riemer, 58–73. New York: Schocken, 1974.

——. *The Ineffable Name of God: Man. Poems in Yiddish and English*. New York: Continuum, 2007.

Hilsenrath, Edgar. *Jossel Wassermans Heimkehr* (*Jossel Wasserman's Return*). Munich: Piper, 1993.

Holloway, Richard. *Waiting for the Last Bus: Reflections on Life and Death*. Edinburgh: Canongate, 2018.

Horn, Dara. *The World to Come*. New York: W. W. Norton, 2006.

Howe, Irving. *World of Our Fathers: Journey of the Eastern European Jews to America*. New York: Harcourt, Brace, Jovanovich, 1976.

Hufford, Mary, Marjorie Hunt, and Steve Zeitlin. *The Grand Generation*. Washington DC: Smithsonian Institution, 1987.

Ignatow, David. *Against the Evidence: Selected Poems 1934–1994*. Middletown CT: Wesleyan University Press, 1994.

Jaffe, Nina, and Steve Zeitlin. *While Standing on One Foot: Puzzle Stories and Wisdom Tales from Jewish Tradition*. New York: Henry Holt, 1993.

Kaminsky, Marc. *A Table with People*. New York: Sun, 1981.

Kaminsky, Marc, and Leon Supraner. *Daily Bread*. Champaign: University of Illinois Press, 1982.

Kaplan, Edward. *Abraham Joshua Heschel: Mind, Heart, Soul*. Philadelphia: Jewish Publication Society, 2019.

Kaufman, Walter A. *Critique of Religion and Philosophy*. Princeton NJ: Princeton University Press, 1979.

Kirshenblatt, Mayer, and Barbara Kirshenblatt-Gimblett. *They Called Me Mayer July: Painted Memories of a Jewish Childhood in Poland before the Holocaust*. Berkeley: University of California Press, 2007.

Kirshenblatt-Gimblett, Barbara. *Traditional Storytelling in the Toronto Jewish Community: A Study in Performance and Creativity in an Immigrant Culture*. Bloomington: Indiana University Proquest, 1972.

Kravitz, Leonard, and Kerry M. Olitzky. *Pirke Avot: A Modern Commentary on Jewish Ethics*. New York: UAHC, 1993.

Kugelmass, Jack. *Miracle on Intervale Avenue*. New York: Columbia University Press, 1996.

Kushner, Lawrence. *The Book of Letters: A Mystical Alef-bait*. Woodstock VT: Jewish Lights, 1990.

——. *God Was in This Place and I, I Did Not Know*. Woodstock VT: Jewish Lights, 2016.

Learsi, Rufus. *Filled with Laughter: A Fiesta of Jewish Folk Humor*. New York: Thomas Yoseloff, 1966.

Lloyd, Timothy. *What Folklorists Do: Professional Possibilities in Folklore Studies*. Bloomington: Indiana University Press, 2021.

Milgram, Goldie, and Ellen Frankel. *Mitzvah Stories: Seeds for Inspiration and Learning*. New Rochelle NY: Reclaiming Judaism, 2011.

Novak, William, and Moshe Waldoks, eds. *The Big Book of Jewish Humor*. New York: William Morrow, 2006.

Oberman, Sheldon. *Solomon and the Ant: And Other Jewish Folktales*. Honesdale PA: Boyds Mills, 2006.

Ornstein, Dan. *Cain v. Abel: A Jewish Courtroom Drama*. Philadelphia: Jewish Publication Society, 2020.

Pastan, Linda. *Aspects of Eve*. New York: Liveright, 1970.

——. *The Five Stages of Grief*. New York: W. W. Norton, 1978.

Peretz, I. L. *The I. L. Peretz Reader*. Translated by Ruth Wisse. New Haven CT: Yale University Press, 2002.

Riemer, Jack. *Jewish Reflections on Death*. New York: Schocken, 1974.

Rossel, Seymour. *The Essential Jewish Stories: God, Torah, Israel & Faith*. Dallas: Rossel, 2018.

Rosten, Leo. *The Joys of Yiddish*. New York: McGraw-Hill, 1968.

Samuel, Maurice. *Little Did I Know: Recollections and Reflections*. New York: Alfred Knopf, 1963.

Schank, Roger. *Tell Me a Story: Narrative and Intelligence*. Evanston IL: Northwestern University Press, 1995.

Scherman, Nosson. *Complete ArtScroll Siddur*. Brooklyn NY: Mesorah, 1984.

Scheub, Harold. *The Poem in the Story: Music, Poetry and Narrative*. Madison: University of Wisconsin Press, 2002.

Schram, Peninnah, ed. *Chosen Tales: Stories Told by Jewish Storytellers*. New York: Jason Aronson, 1995.

——. *The Hungry Clothes and Other Jewish Folktales*. New York: Sterling, 2008.

——. *Jewish Stories One Generation Tells Another*. New York: Jason Aronson, 1987.

——. *Stories within Stories: From the Jewish Oral Tradition*. New York: Jason Aronson, 2000.

———. *Tales of Elijah the Prophet*. New York: Jason Aronson, 1991.

Schram, Peninnah, and Rachayl Eckstein Davis. *The Apple Tree's Discovery*. Minneapolis: Kar Ben, 2012.

Schram, Peninnah, and Sandy Eisenberg Sasso. *Jewish Stories of Love and Marriage: Folktales, Legends and Letters*. New York: Rowman & Littlefield, 2015.

Schwartz, Cherie Karo. *Circle Spinning: Jewish Turning and Returning Tales*. Aurora CO: Hamsa, 2002.

Schwartz, Howard. *Gabriel's Palace*. New York: Oxford University Press, 1993.

———. *Palace of Pearls: The Stories of Rabbi Nachman of Bratslav*. London: Oxford University Press, 2018.

———. *Tree of Souls: The Mythology of Judaism*. London: Oxford University Press, 2004.

Schwarz, Renée Fodor. *Renée*. New York: Shengold, 1991.

Schwartz, Richard H. *Jews and Vegetarianism*. New York: Lantern, 2001.

Schwartz-Bart, André. *The Last of the Just*. New York: Overlook, 1959.

Sholem Aleichem. *Tevye the Dairyman and the Railroad Stories*. New York: Schocken, 1996.

Shuman, Amy. *Other People's Stories*: *Entitlement Claims and the Critique of Empathy*. Champagne: University of Illinois Press, 2010.

Siegel, Danny. *Radiance: Creative Mitzvah Living*. Philadelphia: Jewish Publication Society, 2020.

Sigalow, Emily. *American JewBu: Jews, Buddhists, and Religious Change*. Princeton NJ: Princeton University Press, 2019.

Simon, Solomon. *The Wise Men of Helm and Their Merry Tales*. Millburn NJ: Behrman House, 1945.

Sirowitz, Hal. *Mother Said*. New York: Crown, 1996.

Solomon, Mark. *My True Body*. New York: Havel Havulim, 2016.

Sparrow. *America: A Prophecy: The Sparrow Reader*. New York: Soft Skull, 2005.

Stein, Joseph. *Fiddler on the Roof: Based on Sholom Aleichem's Stories*. New York: Limelight, 2004.

Sweeney, Julia. *If It's Not One Thing, It's Your Mother*. New York: Simon & Schuster, 2014.

Teutsch, David, ed. *Kol Haneshamah: Limot Hol—The Daily Prayer Book*. Wyncote PA: Reconstructionist, 1996.

Ueland, Brenda. *If You Want to Write*. Eastford CT: Martino, 2011.

Umansky, Ellen M., and Diane Ashton. *Four Centuries of Jewish Women's Spirituality: A Sourcebook*. Boston: Beacon, 1992.

Weissler, Chava. *Voices of the Matriarchs*. Boston: Beacon, 1999.

Wex, Michael. *Rhapsody in Schmaltz: Yiddish Food and Why We Can't Stop Eating It.* New York: St. Martin's, 2016.

Wiesel, Elie. *Gates of the Forest.* Translated from the French by Frances Frenaye. New York: Holt, Rinehart & Winston, 1966.

—— . *Sages and Dreamers: Biblical, Talmudic, and Hasidic Portraits and Legends.* New York: Touchstone, 1993.

—— . *Souls on Fire: Portraits and Legends of Hasidic Masters.* New York: Simon & Schuster, 1972.

Yolen, Jane. *Favorite Folktales from around the World.* New York: Pantheon, 1986.

Zborowski, Mark, and Elizabeth Herzog. *Life Is with People.* New York: Schocken, 1995.

Zeiger, Lila. *The Way to Castle Garden.* Pittsford NY: State Street, 1982.

Zeitlin, Aaron. *Poems of the Holocaust and Poems of Faith.* Translated by Morris F. Faierstein. Lincoln NE: iUniverse, 2007.

Zeitlin, Steve. *Because God Loves Stories: An Anthology of Jewish Storytelling.* New York: Simon & Schuster, 1997.

COMMENTATOR BIOGRAPHIES

ROBERT J. BERNSTEIN is an acclaimed autism specialist and therapist. He is the author of *Uniquely Normal: Tapping the Reservoir of Normalcy to Treat Autism* with a foreword by Dr. Temple Grandin. His work offers a new approach to cognitive thinking: to assist people with ASD to be able to live in the world and connect with the people in it as themselves, expressing their unique humanity and engaging more fully in the human interactions that give life meaning.

ESTHER COHEN (esthercohen.com) writes, teaches, and is a cultural activist. She posts a poem every single day at Overheardec@substack.com, perhaps owning a world's record in that regard. She served as director of Bread and Roses, the cultural arm of union 1199SEIU. She is the author of six books, including *Book Doctor*, based, in part, on tireless efforts to edit and encourage writers.

LISA LIPKIN is a professional storyteller and writer who has performed her work across the United States and beyond. She is the founder of Story Strategies (storystrategies .net), a consultancy that helps organizations ranging from Shell Oil to the Museum of the City of New York, showing them how to use the power of narrative to persuade and engage listeners. Her articles and stories have appeared in the *New York Times Magazine* and *The New Yorker*, among others.

BOB MANKOFF submitted more than five hundred cartoons to *The New Yorker* for over two years before he had his first one published. He is the former cartoon editor of the magazine and president of Cartoon Collections, a cartoon licensing database. One of his cartoons (captioned "No, Thursday's out. How about never—is never good for you?") is one of *The New Yorker*'s most widely reprinted cartoons. He has served as a mentor to hundreds of cartoonists.

FLASH ROSENBERG draws, photographs, writes, and performs. She is a Guggenheim Fellow in the Creative Arts, a mainstage storyteller for The Moth, and a translator of complex concepts into instant drawings for major clients, such as Visa, Gatorade, the nation of Mexico, Verizon, the Ford Foundation, and the United Nations. Flash Rosenberg Studio is a full-service photography, motion picture, merriment, and mischief factory based in New York City. She lives with two turtles and infinite questions.

JACK SANTINO is professor emeritus of popular culture at Bowling Green State University and former director of the Bowling Green Center for Culture Studies. He is the author of numerous books and articles on ritual, celebrations, and holidays, including *Public Performances: Studies in the Carnivalesque and the Ritualesque*. Along with Paul Wagner, Santino produced the Emmy Award–winning documentary, *Miles of Smiles, Years of Struggle*, a film about the history of the African American Pullman Porters. He is a former editor of the *Journal of American Folklore* and past president of the American Folklore Society.

RABBI EDWARD SCHECTER has been rabbi of Temple Beth Shalom in Hastings-on-Hudson, New York, for fifty years. Ordained at the Hebrew Union College-Jewish Institute of Religion, he has completed graduate studies in Jewish history at CUNY, Hebrew literature at NYU, city management at the University of Cincinnati, and early childhood at Sarah Lawrence College. He is currently on the board of Kivunim, an Israel-based gap-year program founded by Peter Geffen. Most of all he likes telling stories.

PENINNAH SCHRAM, the lead commentator for *JEWels*, is professor emerita at Yeshiva University. She is an internationally known storyteller and the author of thirteen books of Jewish folktales, including *Jewish Stories One Generation Tells Another* and *Stories within Stories: From the Jewish Oral Tradition*. She is the recipient of the National Storytellers Network 2003 Lifetime Achievement Award. Most recently, author Caren Neile published *Peninnah's World: A Jewish Life in Stories*, about Peninnah's life transitions leading to her becoming a storyteller and helping to revive the Jewish storytelling tradition.

ZEV SHANKEN is the former literary editor of *Response: A Contemporary Jewish Review* and has contributed to *Bantam's Jewish Almanac* and Richard Light's *Jewish Rites of Death*. With Richard Siegel he originated, researched, and developed *How to Be a Perfect Stranger: The Essential Religious Etiquette Handbook* for Jewish Lights Publishing. A former high school English teacher, he is the author of two books of original poetry, *Memory Tricks* and *If I Try to Be Like Him, Who Will Be Like Me?*

STEVE ZEITLIN received his PhD in folklore and folklife from the University of Pennsylvania and an MA in literature from Bucknell University. He is the founding director of City Lore, New York's center for urban folk culture. He is the codirector of a number of documentary films, including *Free Show Tonight* on traveling medicine shows, and author of ten books on America's folk culture, including *Because God Loves Stories: An Anthology of Jewish Storytelling*, *The Poetry of Everyday Life: Storytelling and the Art of Awareness*, as well as a volume of poetry, *I Hear America Singing in the Rain*.

INDEX